'LAKELAND I

BOOK 2 — THE NORTH AND EAST

This guide book, which is the second of a se
contains exact, but simple directions for the n
to such well known places as Keswick, Butterm
an exploration of the quieter valleys, fells ai   ...... u. ims outstandingly
beautiful area.

The Main Circle Route (Maps 1-13), shown on the Key Map opposite covers 120 miles and is far too long for a leisurely day's journey. We have therefore included 'link routes' to break this up into smaller circles (see Key Map). Each route, being circular, may of course be started at any point suitable to you.

HOW TO USE YOUR BOOK ON THE ROUTE

Each double page makes up a complete picture of the country ahead of you. On the left you will find a one inch to the mile strip map, with the route marked by a series of dashes. Direction is always from top to bottom, so that the map may be looked at in conjunction with the 'directions to the driver', with which it is cross referenced by a letter itemising each junction point. This enables the driver to have exact guidance every time an opportunity for changing direction occurs, even if it is only "Keep straight, not left!".

With mileage intervals shown, the driver should even have warning when to expect those 'moments of decision', and if a sign post exists we have used this to help you, with 'Follow sign marked...' column. However re-signing is always in progress, and this may lead to slight differences in sign marking in some cases...So beware of freshly erected signs.

We have also included a description of the towns and villages through which you will pass, together with some photographs to illustrate the route.

To gain full enjoyment from your journeys be prepared to leave your car as often as possible. We have tried to lead you away from the busy main road whenever possible, but in constricted mountain country this is not always easy to achieve. We have referred briefly in the text to the dangers of attempting remote hill walks, or climbing of any sort, without adequate experience or equipment, but if at the moment you possess neither, be not dismayed, for it is still possible to find the solitude enjoyed by earlier generations of visitors, by walking only a few hundred yards away from the roadside. Many of you will then wish to become more adventurous, and this is the time to seek further advice. May we suggest that you first call at the National Park Centre, Brockhole (page 23) for advice. Then if possible purchase one or more of the classic Guides to the Lakeland Fells, by Mr. A. Wainright, or *The Lakeland Peaks* by Mr. W. A. Poucher. The new 1:25,000 series of Ordnance Survey Maps are another essential requisite.

Do not try to cover too many road miles in one day, for there are so many wonderful opportunities for enjoyment for those who are really prepared to look about them...sweeping bracken covered fells, sombre mountain tops, delicious lake shores, mountain tarns, quiet woodlands and sparkling streams. So drive slowly, stop often, and take time off to absorb the splendours of this unique landscape.

COMPILED BY PETER AND HELEN TITCHMARSH
REVISED BY ALLAN AND IRENE BLACKNALL
PHOTOGRAPHY BY ALAN AND PETER TITCHMARSH

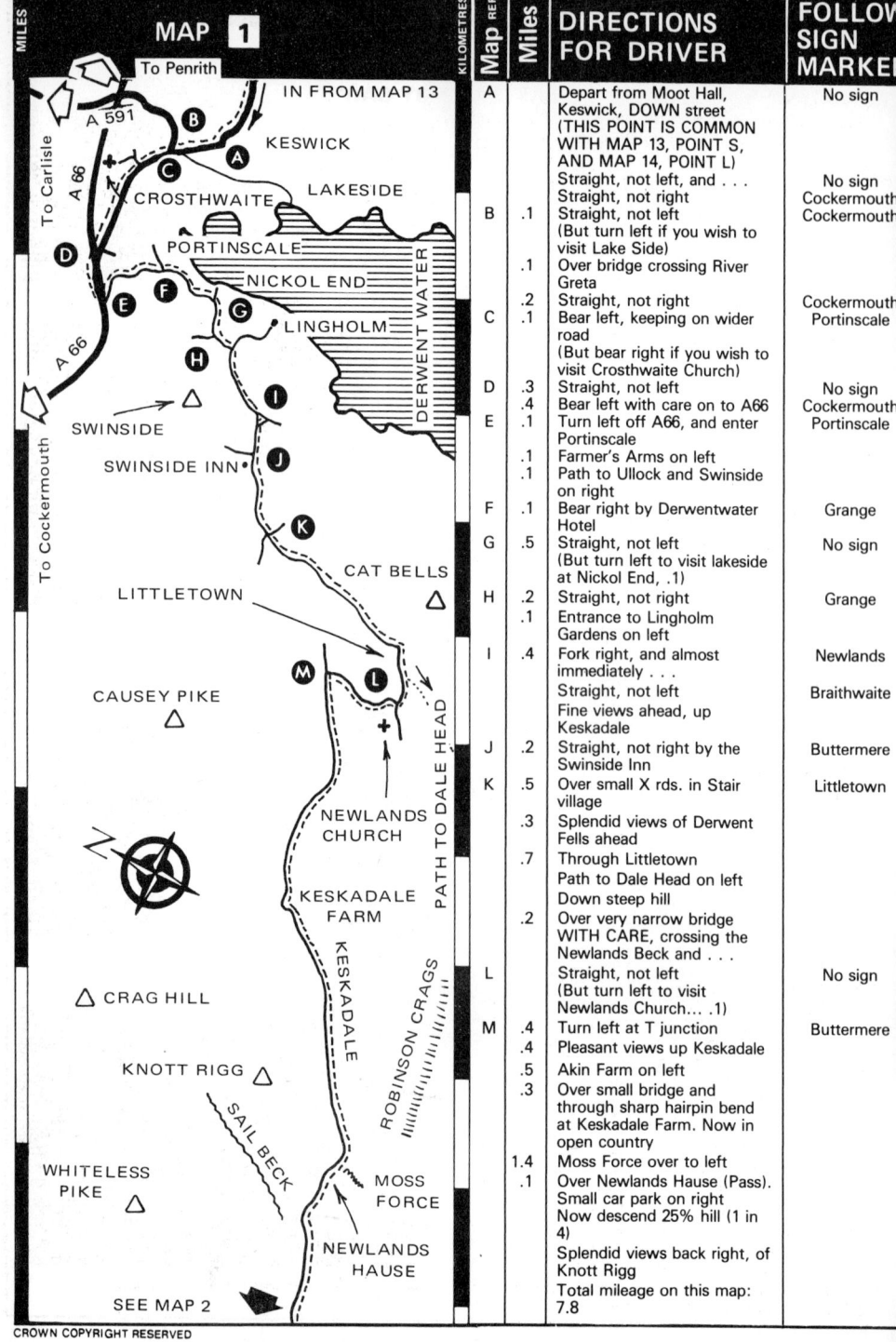

MAP 1

Map REF	Miles	DIRECTIONS FOR DRIVER	FOLLOW SIGN MARKED
A		Depart from Moot Hall, Keswick, DOWN street (THIS POINT IS COMMON WITH MAP 13, POINT S, AND MAP 14, POINT L) Straight, not left, and . . .	No sign
		Straight, not right	No sign Cockermouth
B	.1	Straight, not left (But turn left if you wish to visit Lake Side)	Cockermouth
	.1	Over bridge crossing River Greta	
	.2	Straight, not right	Cockermouth
C	.1	Bear left, keeping on wider road (But bear right if you wish to visit Crosthwaite Church)	Portinscale
D	.3	Straight, not left	No sign
	.4	Bear left with care on to A66	Cockermouth
E	.1	Turn left off A66, and enter Portinscale	Portinscale
	.1	Farmer's Arms on left	
	.1	Path to Ullock and Swinside on right	
F	.1	Bear right by Derwentwater Hotel	Grange
G	.5	Straight, not left (But turn left to visit lakeside at Nickol End, .1)	No sign
H	.2	Straight, not right	Grange
	.1	Entrance to Lingholm Gardens on left	
I	.4	Fork right, and almost immediately . . .	Newlands
		Straight, not left	Braithwaite
		Fine views ahead, up Keskadale	
J	.2	Straight, not right by the Swinside Inn	Buttermere
K	.5	Over small X rds. in Stair village	Littletown
	.3	Splendid views of Derwent Fells ahead	
	.7	Through Littletown Path to Dale Head on left Down steep hill	
	.2	Over very narrow bridge WITH CARE, crossing the Newlands Beck and . . .	
L		Straight, not left (But turn left to visit Newlands Church... .1)	No sign
M	.4	Turn left at T junction	Buttermere
	.4	Pleasant views up Keskadale	
	.5	Akin Farm on left	
	.3	Over small bridge and through sharp hairpin bend at Keskadale Farm. Now in open country	
	1.4	Moss Force over to left	
	.1	Over Newlands Hause (Pass). Small car park on right Now descend 25% hill (1 in 4)	
		Splendid views back right, of Knott Rigg	
		Total mileage on this map: 7.8	

CROWN COPYRIGHT RESERVED

PLACES OF INTEREST ON THE ROUTE

Keswick

Busy and attractive northern centre of Lakeland, lying at the south end of lovely Derwentwater and backed by the great mass of Skiddaw and Blencathra. It has a wide selection of hotels, guest houses, inns, shops and restaurants; and centres upon its minute Moot Hall, built in 1813, and most effectively restored in 1971. (Now used as an Information Centre.) See also the interesting Cumberland Pencil Museum, and the Fitz Park Museum and Art Gallery, with its well known collection of manuscripts by various Lakeland authors and poets. Visit the 'Lake Side', where there is a large car park, from whence one can walk to Friar's Crag, a fine viewpoint over the lake, hire a boat, or go for a cruise. Another well known viewpoint is Castle Head, which lies in woodland behind Friar's Crag.

1. Lake Side, Keswick

Crosthwaite Church

A large 16th century building in a beautiful churchyard, with fine views of Grisedale Pike and Catbells to the south and west. The church has a large interior, the contents of which includes an interesting 14th century font, and a memorial to Robert Southey in white marble.

Portinscale

Bright little village, with an attractive inn, the Farmer's Arms, and an equally pleasant hotel, The Derwentwater.

Nickol End

An agreeable lakeside spot, with motor, rowing and sailing boats for hire. Car parking space very limited.

2. Crosthwaite Church

Lingholm Gardens

Beautifully maintained gardens with rhododendrons and azaleas, and extensive woodlands. There are fine views out across Derwentwater to the Borrowdale Fells. Well worth visiting.

Littletown

Unspoilt hamlet below Catbells peak, with entrancing views out over the Newlands valley, and down the valley to Skiddaw.

Newlands Church

Small, white painted 'dale chapel', with miniature school attached. It was re-built in 1843, but contains a Jacobean pulpit and reading desk, and some panelling which certainly looks older than the 19th century pews. This is a pleasing little building, in a most attractive setting, with views up the Newland Beck towards High Spy.

3. Newlands Valley, beyond Littletown

Keskadale and Newlands Hause

An exceptionally beautiful valley, with fine views from our road of great sweeping mountain sides, dropping down to the little Keskadale Beck. We are overlooked by Robinson over to our left, and Knott Rigg above us to the right. The great crags of Robinson finally come to an end at the pass of Newlands Hause (sometimes referred to as Buttermere Hause). This is overlooked on our left by the high waterfall of Moss Force.

4. Sail Beck, below Newlands Hause

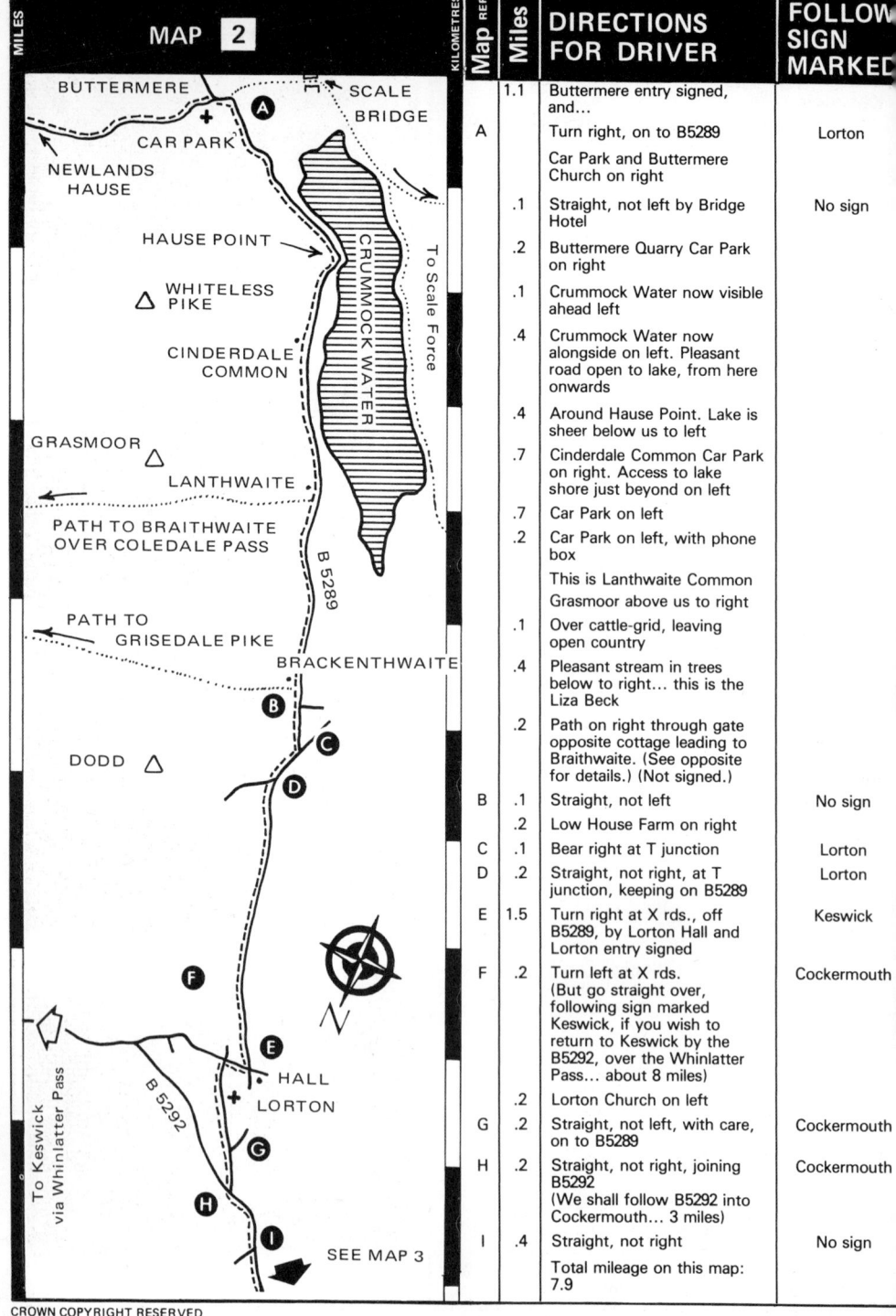

Map REF	Miles	DIRECTIONS FOR DRIVER	FOLLOW SIGN MARKED
	1.1	Buttermere entry signed, and...	
A		Turn right, on to B5289	Lorton
		Car Park and Buttermere Church on right	
	.1	Straight, not left by Bridge Hotel	No sign
	.2	Buttermere Quarry Car Park on right	
	.1	Crummock Water now visible ahead left	
	.4	Crummock Water now alongside on left. Pleasant road open to lake, from here onwards	
	.4	Around Hause Point. Lake is sheer below us to left	
	.7	Cinderdale Common Car Park on right. Access to lake shore just beyond on left	
	.7	Car Park on left	
	.2	Car Park on left, with phone box	
		This is Lanthwaite Common Grasmoor above us to right	
	.1	Over cattle-grid, leaving open country	
	.4	Pleasant stream in trees below to right... this is the Liza Beck	
	.2	Path on right through gate opposite cottage leading to Braithwaite. (See opposite for details.) (Not signed.)	
B	.1	Straight, not left	No sign
	.2	Low House Farm on right	
C	.1	Bear right at T junction	Lorton
D	.2	Straight, not right, at T junction, keeping on B5289	Lorton
E	1.5	Turn right at X rds., off B5289, by Lorton Hall and Lorton entry signed	Keswick
F	.2	Turn left at X rds. (But go straight over, following sign marked Keswick, if you wish to return to Keswick by the B5292, over the Whinlatter Pass... about 8 miles)	Cockermouth
	.2	Lorton Church on left	
G	.2	Straight, not left, with care, on to B5289	Cockermouth
H	.2	Straight, not right, joining B5292 (We shall follow B5292 into Cockermouth... 3 miles)	Cockermouth
I	.4	Straight, not right	No sign
		Total mileage on this map: 7.9	

CROWN COPYRIGHT RESERVED

PLACES OF INTEREST ON THE ROUTE

Buttermere
Small village with hotel, guest houses and petrol station. The little church, with its typically 19th century interior is charmingly sited on a slope overlooking the village.

Scale Force
Walk south west from Buttermere village, over Scale Bridge, crossing the River Dubs, which flows from Buttermere into Crummock Water. Then turn right and follow the Dubs, and the Crummock shoreline, before turning up left into the Scale Beck valley. Scale Force will be found, set in a wooded ravine, leaping 120 feet sheer into a small pool. (Distance from Buttermere, about 2 miles.)

Sour Milk Gill
One of many waterfalls with this title, this one comes down the mountainside from Bleaberry Tarn, and can best be reached by turning left immediately after crossing Scale Bridge.

Crummock Water
Large lake (2½ miles long) overlooked by the dramatic, conical peak of Mellbreak in the west, with Grasmoor and Whiteless Pike to the east. There is a path along its western shore (from Buttermere, via Scale Bridge) to Kirkstile (see Book 1).

Cinderdale Common
A pleasantly open area, with access to Crummock Water shore for walkers, and quiet picnic places overlooking the water, not far from our road.

Lanthwaite Green
Another open area with reasonable parking facilities, and splendid views back to Crummock Water. Grasmoor is above us to the right; Mellbreak with its great screes is over beyond Crummock Water; while Great Gable is far back to the south. There is a path to the east from here, to Coledale Pass, from whence Grasmoor can be tackled.

Brackenthwaite
There is a path eastwards from here (cottage with gate opposite...see Route Directions) up over Whiteside, Hobcarton Pike, down to Braithwaite.

Lorton Hall
A largely 17th century manor house, incorporating a medieval Pele Tower (see page 7), and set in ornamental gardens.

Whinlatter Pass
See Route Directions at Point F, if you wish to return to Keswick over the Whinlatter Pass. This is one of Lakeland's simplest passes, and there is an interesting Visitor Centre run by the Forestry Commission at its eastern end, above Braithwaite.

Lorton Church
An early 19th century Gothic building, with a white painted interior containing little of interest. The large churchyard contains many attractively carved monuments, and we particularly liked the short inscription on Daniel Fisher's reading —
*On tombstones praise is vainly spent,
Good works is man's best monument.*

1. Our road down to Buttermere

2. Buttermere Church

3. Crummock Water

4. Lanthwaite Green

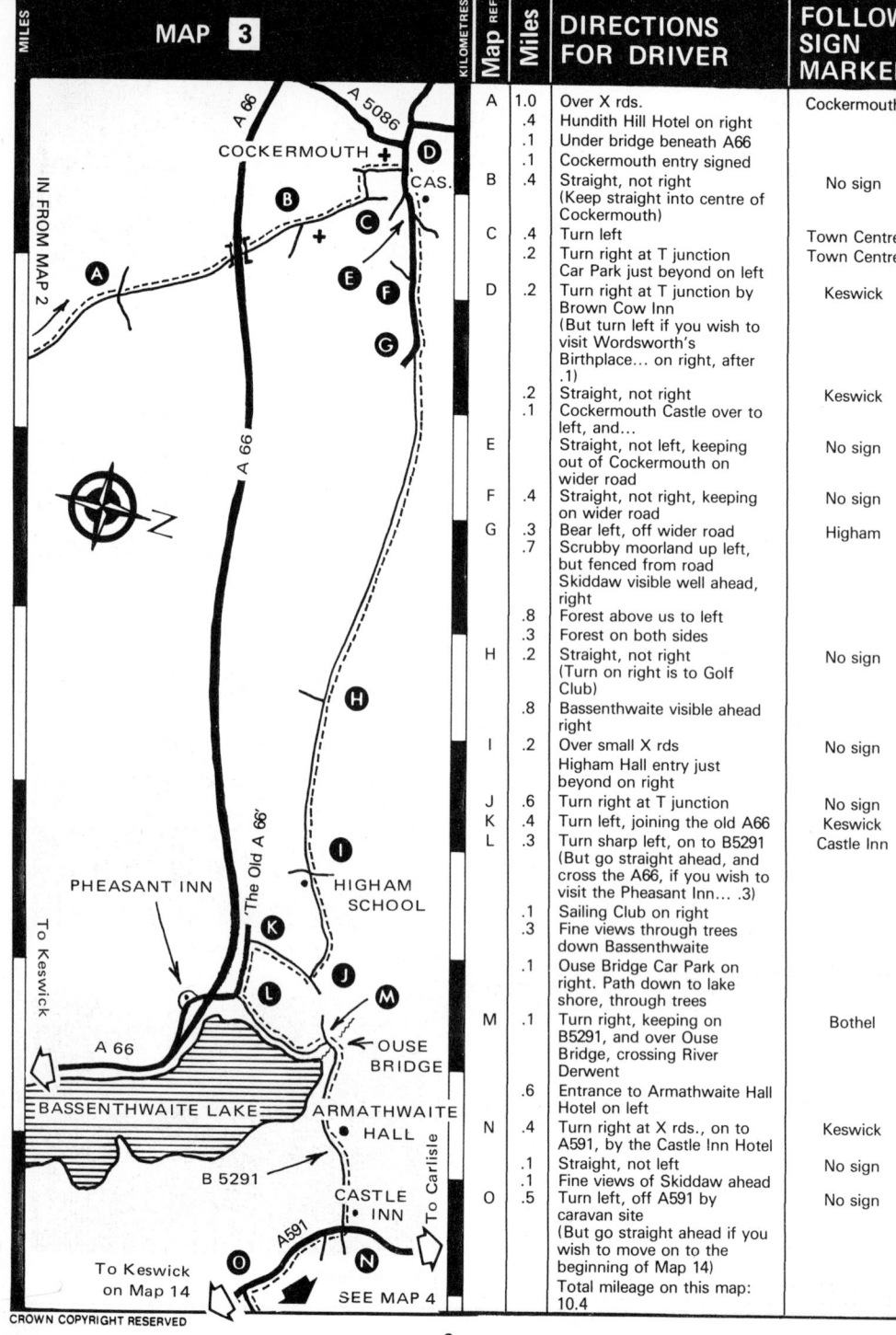

MAP 3

Map REF	Miles	DIRECTIONS FOR DRIVER	FOLLOW SIGN MARKED
A	1.0	Over X rds.	Cockermouth
	.4	Hundith Hill Hotel on right	
	.1	Under bridge beneath A66	
	.1	Cockermouth entry signed	
B	.4	Straight, not right (Keep straight into centre of Cockermouth)	No sign
C	.4	Turn left	Town Centre
	.2	Turn right at T junction Car Park just beyond on left	Town Centre
D	.2	Turn right at T junction by Brown Cow Inn (But turn left if you wish to visit Wordsworth's Birthplace... on right, after .1)	Keswick
	.2	Straight, not right	Keswick
	.1	Cockermouth Castle over to left, and...	
E		Straight, not left, keeping out of Cockermouth on wider road	No sign
F	.4	Straight, not right, keeping on wider road	No sign
G	.3	Bear left, off wider road	Higham
	.7	Scrubby moorland up left, but fenced from road Skiddaw visible well ahead, right	
	.8	Forest above us to left	
	.3	Forest on both sides	
H	.2	Straight, not right (Turn on right is to Golf Club)	No sign
	.8	Bassenthwaite visible ahead right	
I	.2	Over small X rds Higham Hall entry just beyond on right	No sign
J	.6	Turn right at T junction	No sign
K	.4	Turn left, joining the old A66	Keswick
L	.3	Turn sharp left, on to B5291 (But go straight ahead, and cross the A66, if you wish to visit the Pheasant Inn... .3)	Castle Inn
	.1	Sailing Club on right	
	.3	Fine views through trees down Bassenthwaite	
	.1	Ouse Bridge Car Park on right. Path down to lake shore, through trees	
M	.1	Turn right, keeping on B5291, and over Ouse Bridge, crossing River Derwent	Bothel
	.6	Entrance to Armathwaite Hall Hotel on left	
N	.4	Turn right at X rds., on to A591, by the Castle Inn Hotel	Keswick
	.1	Straight, not left	No sign
	.1	Fine views of Skiddaw ahead	
O	.5	Turn left, off A591 by caravan site (But go straight ahead if you wish to move on to the beginning of Map 14)	No sign
		Total mileage on this map: 10.4	

CROWN COPYRIGHT RESERVED

PLACES OF INTEREST ON THE ROUTE

Cockermouth
In no way a typical Lakeland town, Cockermouth is nevertheless worth visiting (try to pick a good sunny day. Cockermouth on a wet afternoon is a formidable experience). Its stout, largely 14th century castle overlooks the confluence of the Rivers Cocker and Derwent, and its grounds are open to the public. At the opposite (western) end of the long Main Street, well beyond the impressive statue of the Sixth Earl of Mayo, stands Wordsworth's birthplace.

This is a handsome 18th century building, in which William Wordsworth was born in 1770, his father being steward to Sir James Lowther, who owned most of the nearby Cumberland coalfields. The house now belongs to the National Trust, and has a most interesting interior, including the original staircase, fireplaces and panelling. Beside the house there is a little lane leading down to the riverside (walkers only), with views of the castle and the old brewery. We also liked the recently erected bust of Wordsworth on a plinth, in a little garden across the street from his birthplace.

1. Wordsworth's Birthplace, Cockermouth

The Pheasant Inn (A Diversion)
Go straight at Point L if you wish to visit the Pheasant Inn, an agreeable hotel and restaurant beyond on the right. Boats may be hired a short distance further on, on the shores of Bassenthwaite. The busy A66 follows much of the western shore of Bassenthwaite, and makes a fast return route to Keswick. However we hope that you will be able to spare the time to follow round to the north of the lake and reach Keswick by way of Map 14...a far quieter and a much more interesting route.

2. Cockermouth Castle

Bassenthwaite Lake
A lovely expanse of water overlooked by Skiddaw on the east and the Lord's Seat on the west. The northern end is, by comparison, flat and open, and through it meanders the River Derwent, which flows out of the lake a few yards above Ouse Bridge, a handsome early 19th century structure, with three fine stone arches. There is a car park on the right, just before the bridge, and from here one can walk down to the quiet tree bordered shore. There are entrancing views from here across the water to Skiddaw, with sailing dinghies, usually adding a touch of colour and movement.

3. Bassenthwaite and Skiddaw

Armathwaite Hall
Large 19th century neo-Tudor mansion, now an hotel.

Pele Towers — A General Note
These were small self contained defensive keeps, usually of three storeys, confined in this form to the county of Cumbria, and several of which are encountered on our route. Cattle were brought into the ground floor as protection against Scots cattle raiders. Most surviving pele towers have been incorporated into larger houses, usually by combining them with a medieval hall.

4. Ouse Bridge

MAP 4

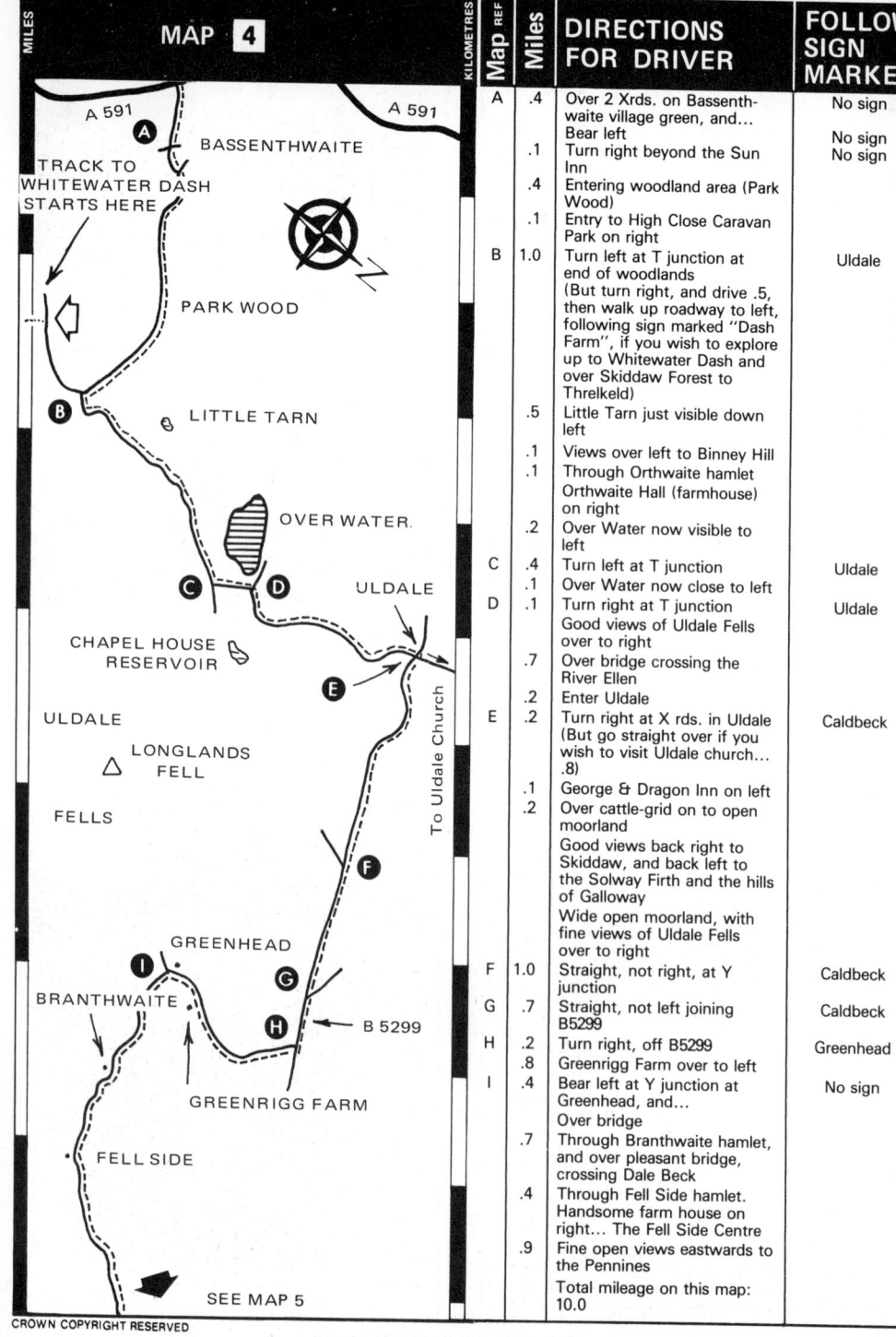

Map REF	Miles	DIRECTIONS FOR DRIVER	FOLLOW SIGN MARKED
A	.4	Over 2 Xrds. on Bassenthwaite village green, and... Bear left	No sign
	.1	Turn right beyond the Sun Inn	No sign
	.4	Entering woodland area (Park Wood)	
	.1	Entry to High Close Caravan Park on right	
B	1.0	Turn left at T junction at end of woodlands (But turn right, and drive .5, then walk up roadway to left, following sign marked "Dash Farm", if you wish to explore up to Whitewater Dash and over Skiddaw Forest to Threlkeld)	Uldale
	.5	Little Tarn just visible down left	
	.1	Views over left to Binney Hill	
	.1	Through Orthwaite hamlet Orthwaite Hall (farmhouse) on right	
	.2	Over Water now visible to left	
C	.4	Turn left at T junction	Uldale
	.1	Over Water now close to left	
D	.1	Turn right at T junction Good views of Uldale Fells over to right	Uldale
	.7	Over bridge crossing the River Ellen	
	.2	Enter Uldale	
E	.2	Turn right at X rds. in Uldale (But go straight over if you wish to visit Uldale church... .8)	Caldbeck
	.1	George & Dragon Inn on left	
	.2	Over cattle-grid on to open moorland	
		Good views back right to Skiddaw, and back left to the Solway Firth and the hills of Galloway	
		Wide open moorland, with fine views of Uldale Fells over to right	
F	1.0	Straight, not right, at Y junction	Caldbeck
G	.7	Straight, not left joining B5299	Caldbeck
H	.2	Turn right, off B5299	Greenhead
	.8	Greenrigg Farm over to left	
I	.4	Bear left at Y junction at Greenhead, and... Over bridge	No sign
	.7	Through Branthwaite hamlet, and over pleasant bridge, crossing Dale Beck	
	.4	Through Fell Side hamlet. Handsome farm house on right... The Fell Side Centre	
	.9	Fine open views eastwards to the Pennines	
		Total mileage on this map: 10.0	

PLACES OF INTEREST ON THE ROUTE

Bassenthwaite Village
Our route on this map misses both the old and new church (see page 29 for old church). Bassenthwaite's wide green is overlooked by undistinguished council housing, but the Sun Inn, a short distance beyond, appears to make up for any lack of character in the rest of the village.

Park Wood
Attractive forest area in a small valley beyond Bassenthwaite. This is largely a softwood plantation, but many oak and beech trees have been planted near the road-side. There are fine views back, over the village, to Bassenthwaite Lake, and the wooded hillsides of Sale Fell beyond.

1. Park Wood, beyond Bassenthwaite

Whitewater Dash and Skiddaw Forest
(See Route Directions...Point B for details of this diversion.)
Whitewater Dash, or Dash Falls, are impressive waterfalls, at the point where the little Dash Beck pours out of the heights of Skiddaw Forest, into the valley below. The falls lie about 2½ miles from the road, not far from a track (walkers only please). This track then climbs up into Skiddaw Forest (once a Royal hunting preserve, not a forest in the arboreal sense) to Skiddaw House, from whence it is possible to walk south to Threlkeld (page 27), or Millbeck (page 29), about eight miles in each case. Do not undertake this trek without proper experience and equipment.

2. Uldale Church

Orthwaite Hall
It is surprising to find such a stylish 17th century house in remote little Orthwaite hamlet. It has stone mullioned doors and windows and a handsome porch, and could easily be missed if you rush through.

Uldale
This small village lies below the remote Uldale Fells, on the northern frontier of Lakeland. Its wide green is bordered with farmhouses, one of which is particularly attractive, and there is a pleasant inn, the George and Dragon, just beyond. The church lies at Uldale Mill hamlet, almost a mile to the north west. This is a small building, with a good looking little 18th century west doorway, looking down at the little mill house below. The interior also has an 18th century flavour, which is enhanced by an attractive board, with scrolly top, commemorating the gift of one, Thomas Cape, born at Uldale, lived in Paternoster Row, London and died at Henley-on-Thames...not the first, and certainly not the last, of all those who have drifted to the south and east in search of a more prosperous life, and who are alas drifting still.

Fell Side
Another hamlet below the Caldbeck Fells, but this one has a handsome 18th century farmhouse...now used as the "Fellside Centre". There used to be lead and barytes mines in the fells to the south. (Barytes still being mined at Sandbed, south of Caldbeck.)

3. Fell Country above Branthwaite

MAP 5

Map labels: TOWNHEAD, THE HOWK, CALDBECK, HESKET NEWMARKET, MILLHOUSE HAMLET, HIGH ROW, CASTLE SOWERBY CHURCH, HUTTON ROOF

Map REF	Miles	DIRECTIONS FOR DRIVER	FOLLOW SIGN MARKED
A	.1	Turn right at T junction	Caldbeck
B	.5	Turn left at T junction	Upton
	.1	Caldbeck entry signed	
	.1	Bear left at T junction, and . . . Over bridge at Townhead	No sign
C	.2	Turn right at T junction, on to wider road in Caldbeck	No sign
	.2	Straight, not left (But turn left, go over bridge, and immediately beyond, walk up left through small yard if you wish to explore up to the Howk. Path looks private. Enquire locally as it is easy to trespass unwittingly)	Wigton
D		Straight not left again by Old Smithy Gift Shop on left, and Clogger's Shop up to right	No sign
		Oddfellows Inn on left	
	.1	Church on left	
	1.0	Hesket Newmarket entry signed	
E	.2	Turn left at T junction, and . . .	Mungrisdale
		Keep straight, not left, by the Old Crown Inn	No sign
F	.4	Fork left at end of village, keeping on wider road	Millhouse
	1.0	Over bridge, crossing river Caldew, in Millhouse hamlet	
G	.1	Turn right	Haltcliff
H	.7	Turn left at T junction, and almost immediately . . .	Mungrisdale
	.1	Turn right at 2nd T junction	No sign
	.5	Track to Castle Sowerby church on left	
		Fine views over to right of Carrock Fell	
I	1.0	Turn right at X rds.	Hutton Roof
J	.2	Straight, not right	No sign
	.3	Through Hutton Roof hamlet	
	.2	Drop down steeply into the Caldew valley, with fine views of Carrock Fell ahead	
K	.3	Turn right	Haltcliff
L	.3	Turn left at T junction	Hesket Newmarket
	.7	Over cattle-grid on to open moorland	
M	.4	Turn left at T junction by High Row Bridge	Mungrisdale
		Total mileage on this map: 8.7	

CROWN COPYRIGHT RESERVED

PLACES OF INTEREST ON THE ROUTE

Caldbeck

Grey stone village at the very northern tip of Lakeland, with bobbin, cloth and clog making, brewing and mining, lending it an air of prosperity in the 19th century. Today only the clog making survives...don't miss the opportunity to buy a pair from one of Britain's few remaining cloggers, at the fascinating little clogger's shop. However, most visitors are drawn to Caldbeck, by the presence in its churchyard of John Peel's grave. Peel spent all his life in the vicinity of Caldbeck, and his passion for the pursuit of foxes was immortalised in his own lifetime in the song written by his friend J. W. Graves.

John Peel's grave is situated a little to the left of Caldbeck's Norman south doorway, which is approached up a long churchyard path, itself overlooked by a handsome rectory, with pretty 'gothick' windows. The interior of the church has been sympathetically restored, but we were more attracted by the pleasant little bridge over the Caldbeck Beck behind the church. We also liked the minute Midland Bank, on our road just beyond the church, and the A.A. roundel stating 'DISTANCE TO LONDON 301½ MILES'...time was, when virtually every village in the country had one of these, but now the few that remain may be observed as quaint relics of earlier days.

See Route Directions for details of access to the Howk...a fascinating little limestone gorge, complete with swallow holes and the remains of a bobbin mill. DON'T MISS THIS.

1. Caldbeck Church

2. Clogger's Shop Caldbeck

3. John Peel's Grave Caldbeck

Hesket Newmarket

As its name implies, this was once a market centre, but trade has moved elsewhere and Hesket Newmarket has been left to age gracefully. Only the little covered market house (beside the filling station) proclaims its former importance, but there are wide greens reminiscent of Yorkshire, and a sense of unhurried calm, which suits this small village beneath the northern fells.

Castle Sowerby

The long, low white painted church stands beside a farmhouse, at the end of a track about a mile from our road (no cars please). This is a largely Norman building, with 13th century additions. The track to Castle Sowerby from our road leads down into a little wooded valley, and up beyond, and makes a pleasant little expedition for walkers seeking a respite from the wilder fell country.

4. Caldbeck Rectory

Hutton Roof

Scanty hamlet, as windswept as its name seems to imply. There are fine views across the Caldew valley to Carrock Fell.

High Row

Attractive little hamlet on the Carrock Beck, at the edge of open moorland country, sweeping down from West Fell and Carrock Fell.

5. Hesket Newmarket

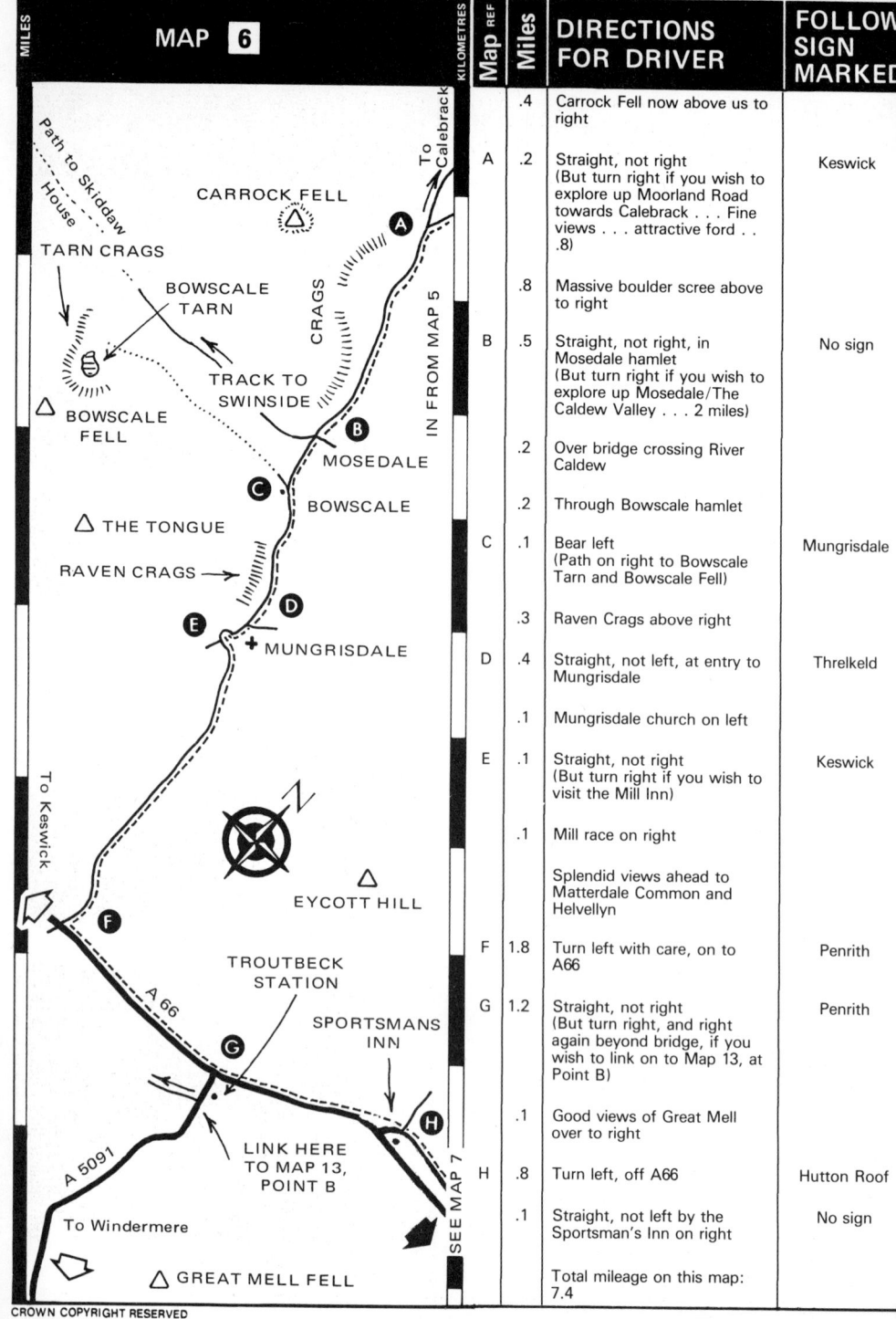

Map REF	Miles	DIRECTIONS FOR DRIVER	FOLLOW SIGN MARKED
	.4	Carrock Fell now above us to right	
A	.2	Straight, not right (But turn right if you wish to explore up Moorland Road towards Calebrack . . . Fine views . . . attractive ford . . .8)	Keswick
	.8	Massive boulder scree above to right	
B	.5	Straight, not right, in Mosedale hamlet (But turn right if you wish to explore up Mosedale/The Caldew Valley . . . 2 miles)	No sign
	.2	Over bridge crossing River Caldew	
	.2	Through Bowscale hamlet	
C	.1	Bear left (Path on right to Bowscale Tarn and Bowscale Fell)	Mungrisdale
	.3	Raven Crags above right	
D	.4	Straight, not left, at entry to Mungrisdale	Threlkeld
	.1	Mungrisdale church on left	
E	.1	Straight, not right (But turn right if you wish to visit the Mill Inn)	Keswick
	.1	Mill race on right	
		Splendid views ahead to Matterdale Common and Helvellyn	
F	1.8	Turn left with care, on to A66	Penrith
G	1.2	Straight, not right (But turn right, and right again beyond bridge, if you wish to link on to Map 13, at Point B)	Penrith
	.1	Good views of Great Mell over to right	
H	.8	Turn left, off A66	Hutton Roof
	.1	Straight, not left by the Sportsman's Inn on right	No sign
		Total mileage on this map: 7.4	

CROWN COPYRIGHT RESERVED

PLACES OF INTEREST ON THE ROUTE

Fell Road towards Calebrack (A diversion)
There are fine views south towards Mungrisdale from this road and a pretty little ford over the Carrock Beck. We have not explored beyond this, to Calebrack, but this should be a reasonable base for motorists who wish to walk up into the 'mining valleys' of the north east fells. (Please refer to A. Wainright's *The Northern Fells*.)

Mosedale
Quiet hamlet from whence there is a path (on right) to Bowscale Fell and Bowscale Tarn. Also turn right here (Point B) for an interesting two mile car journey up Mosedale. This is an attractive road in an area more like Scotland than the Lake District, and is the deepest access into the mountain fastness of the northern fells that the motorist can obtain. After two miles our road becomes a private access to a tungsten mine, but there is a path for walkers that follows the Caldew valley almost to its source near Skiddaw House (see page 9). (Experienced fell walkers only.)
The Caldew valley is also the best access point to Carrock Fell (2174'), which rises above its entrance, about a mile to the north. There are the remains of an extensive Iron Age hill fort encompassing the summit. (Experienced fell walkers only.)

Mungrisdale
Fell-side village with a pleasant inn, and a little white painted 18th century 'dale chapel' church. This has a nave and chancel in one, a minute bellcote, old flagged floors, late 17th century box pews, and a lovely three decker pulpit of the same period. This little building is full of atmosphere, and should certainly not be missed. The Mill Inn, a short distance beyond, still has its mill sluice, and its stream is quite a feature of the latter part of the village. There is a path from Mungrisdale, leading south west, up the valley of the Glenderamackin, and over a shoulder of Scales Fell to Scales hamlet (see page 27).

Link to Map 13
To link to Map 13, turn RIGHT at Point G, leaving A66, and moving on to A5091. Pass the old Troutbeck Station on your left, and turn right beyond the old railway bridge. YOU ARE NOW AT MAP 13, POINT B.

Hutton John (see page 14)
An Elizabethan manor house, having its origins in a pele tower (see page 7). Additions and alterations have been made in the 17th, 18th and 19th centuries, but the essentially Elizabethan flavour of Hutton John survives. There are fine views southwards from the attractive, terraced gardens.

1. The Fells beyond Hutton Roof (See page 10)

2. Our road to Mosedale

3. Bowscale Fell from Point C

4. Mungrisdale Church

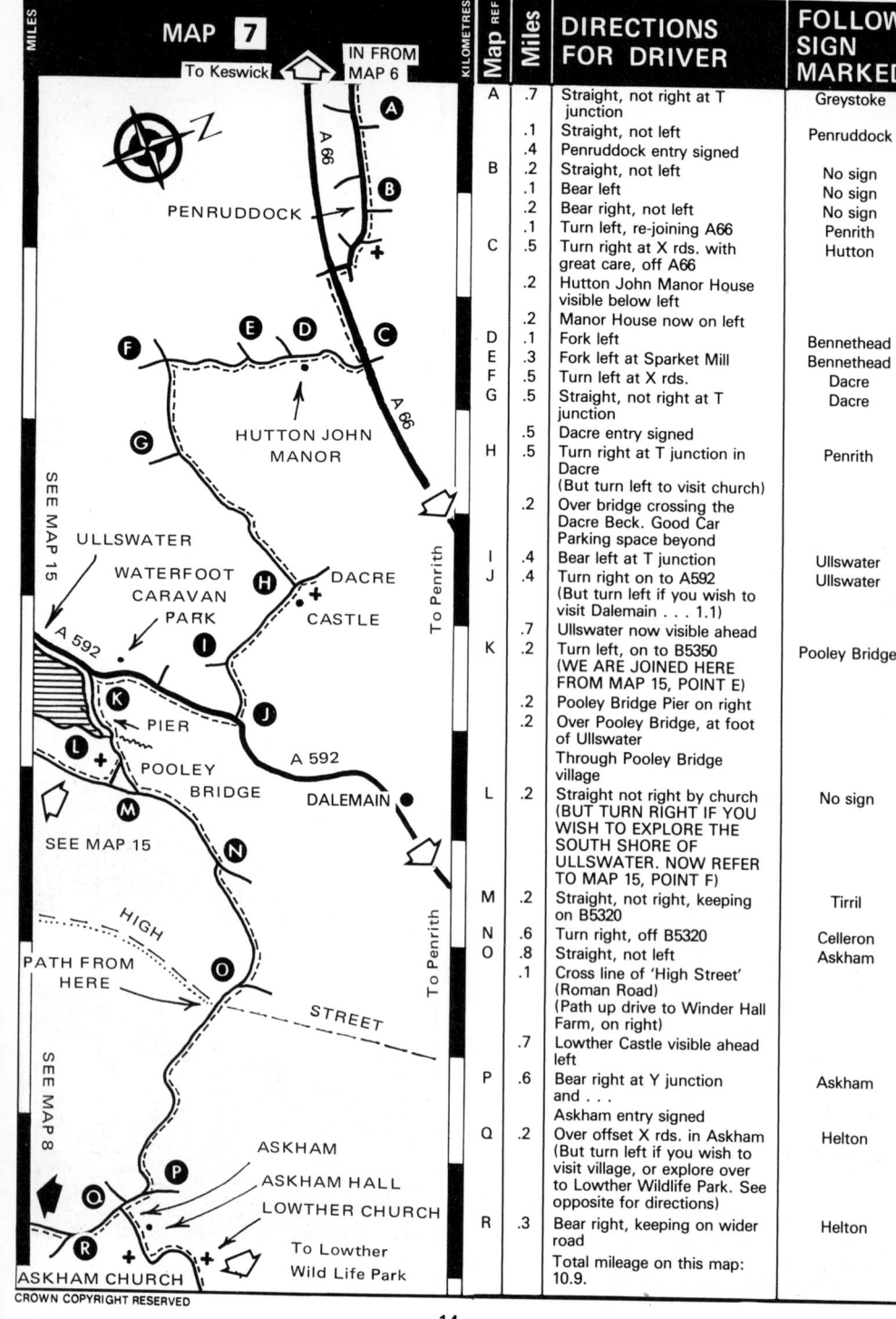

MAP 7 — To Keswick / IN FROM MAP 6

Map Ref	Miles	DIRECTIONS FOR DRIVER	FOLLOW SIGN MARKED
A	.7	Straight, not right at T junction	Greystoke
	.1	Straight, not left	Penruddock
	.4	Penruddock entry signed	
B	.2	Straight, not left	No sign
	.1	Bear left	No sign
	.2	Bear right, not left	No sign
	.1	Turn left, re-joining A66	Penrith
C	.5	Turn right at X rds. with great care, off A66	Hutton
	.2	Hutton John Manor House visible below left	
	.2	Manor House now on left	
D	.1	Fork left	Bennethead
E	.3	Fork left at Sparket Mill	Bennethead
F	.5	Turn left at X rds.	Dacre
G	.5	Straight, not right at T junction	Dacre
	.5	Dacre entry signed	
H	.5	Turn right at T junction in Dacre (But turn left to visit church)	Penrith
	.2	Over bridge crossing the Dacre Beck. Good Car Parking space beyond	
I	.4	Bear left at T junction	Ullswater
J	.4	Turn right on to A592 (But turn left if you wish to visit Dalemain . . . 1.1)	Ullswater
	.7	Ullswater now visible ahead	
K	.2	Turn left, on to B5350 (WE ARE JOINED HERE FROM MAP 15, POINT E)	Pooley Bridge
	.2	Pooley Bridge Pier on right	
	.2	Over Pooley Bridge, at foot of Ullswater	
		Through Pooley Bridge village	
L	.2	Straight not right by church (BUT TURN RIGHT IF YOU WISH TO EXPLORE THE SOUTH SHORE OF ULLSWATER. NOW REFER TO MAP 15, POINT F)	No sign
M	.2	Straight, not right, keeping on B5320	Tirril
N	.6	Turn right, off B5320	Celleron
O	.8	Straight, not left	Askham
	.1	Cross line of 'High Street' (Roman Road) (Path up drive to Winder Hall Farm, on right)	
	.7	Lowther Castle visible ahead left	
P	.6	Bear right at Y junction and . . . Askham entry signed	Askham
Q	.2	Over offset X rds. in Askham (But turn left if you wish to visit village, or explore over to Lowther Wildlife Park. See opposite for directions)	Helton
R	.3	Bear right, keeping on wider road	Helton
		Total mileage on this map: 10.9.	

CROWN COPYRIGHT RESERVED

PLACES OF INTEREST ON THE ROUTE

Hutton John (see page 13)

Dacre
Small village with an interesting church and castle. There are two very interesting fragments of Anglo-Danish cross shafts in the church, and, in complete contrast, a fine monument by Sir Francis Chantrey, with a typically poignant Chantrey figure lamenting by an urn. Do not overlook the strange bears at the four corners of the original churchyard.
The castle, now a manor farm, stands beyond the churchyard, and is in fact a 14th century pele tower (see page 7), with very grand windows added towards the end of the 17th century, NOT OPEN TO THE PUBLIC.

1. Dacre Church   2. Beast at Dacre

Dalemain
A fine medieval, Elizabethan and early Georgian house and gardens set in well wooded parkland. There is an Agricultural Museum, and a Museum devoted to the Westmorland and Cumberland Yeomanry. Countryside Park and Picnic Areas.

Pooley Bridge (see page 31)

High Street (see page 29)

Askham
A most agreeable village with wide greens each side of the road, overlooked by neat stone houses and cottages, with the Queen's Head by the cross roads, and the Punchbowl further down. Askham Hall is based upon a medieval pele tower (see page 7), and can best be viewed back from the road to Lowther (see below). The church was built in 1832 by Robert Smirke, the builder of Lowther Castle, and, more distantly the British Museum. It is surprisingly full of atmosphere, with several tablets to the Sandfords (of Askham Hall) in the south transept.

3. Dalemain

Lowther Church
Fascinating building looking out over the Lowther valley. It is full of architectural mysteries (beyond our scope, we fear), but the series of very grand Lowther/Lonsdale monuments should on no account be missed. Also, do not overlook the strange mausoleum in the churchyard, with a 19th century Earl of Lonsdale in white marble.

4. The Pier at Pooley Bridge

Lowther Castle
The present castle, now a spectacular ruin, was built by Robert Smirke between 1806 and 1811, and was only reduced to its present state in 1957.

Lowther Wildlife Park
(Turn left at Point Q, drive past castle, and then follow signs to Wildlife Park...2.4 miles in total.)
One hundred and fifty acres of splendid parkland, with five species of deer wandering at will. Other animals on view include giant cranes, highland cattle, Jacob sheep, African cattle, flamingoes, otters and a wide variety of birds.

5. Askham

MAP 8

Map features:
- HELTON
- PATH LINKING TO HIGH STREET
- WIDEWATH MILL
- ROUGH HILL FARM
- HULLOCKHOWE
- CROSS GATE
- BAMPTON
- BAMPTON GRANGE
- BOMBY
- DIVERSION TO HAWESWATER
- ROSGILL
- DIVERSION TO SWINDALE
- To Penrith
- SHAP ABBEY
- SHAP
- KELD CHAPEL
- PATH TO MOSEDALE AND GATESGARTH PASS
- A6
- SEE MAP 9

CROWN COPYRIGHT RESERVED

Map Ref	Miles	DIRECTIONS FOR DRIVER	FOLLOW SIGN MARKED
	.5	Helton entry signed	
A	.1	Straight, not right, keeping on wider road, avoiding Helton village	Haweswater
B	.3	Straight not right	No sign
C	.3	Fork right, off wider road (Do not TURN right) (WATCH FOR THIS WITH GREAT CARE)	'Heltondale'
	.3	Over bridge and cattle-grid on to open moorland by Widewath Mill	
	1.2	Over cattle-grid	
	.2	Through gate, and almost immediately . . .	
D		Turn right by Rough Hill Farm buildings, and . . . Through 2nd gate, keeping farm building on LEFT	Bampton
	.1	Through 3rd gate	
	.2	Through 4th gate	
	.1	Through 5th gate, and . . .	
E		Turn left at T junction	No sign
	.3	Past Hullockhowe farms	
	.4	Over cattle-grid	
F	.1	Bear sharp left on common land at Cross Gate Farm	No sign
G	.3	Bear right, on to wider road at entry to Bampton, and . . .	No sign
	.1	Turn left	Shap
H	.3	Bear right at T junction (But turn left if you wish to visit Bampton church)	Haweswater
I	.3	Straight, not right (But turn right to visit Haweswater)	Swindale
	.1	Straight, not right, in Bomby hamlet	No sign
J	.8	Straight, not right (But fork right if you wish to explore up Swindale . . . 3.5 miles)	No sign
	.3	Over bridge crossing River Lowther	
	.1	Through Rosgill hamlet	
K	.5	Bear right, on to wider road	Shap
L	1.2	Turn left at T junction (But turn very sharp right **with great care** if you wish to visit Shap Abbey half a mile)	Shap
M	.2	Turn left at T junction (But turn sharp right if you wish to visit Keld Chapel . . . .7)	Shap
	.1	Shap entry signed	
N	.1	Turn right, on to A6 (Keep on A6 for 11 miles)	Kendal
O	.2	Straight, not left, in Shap (But turn left if you wish to visit church)	Kendal
	.2	Market House on right	
	.4	Greyhound Hotel on left	
		Total mileage on this map: 9.3	

PLACES OF INTEREST ON THE ROUTE

Moorland Route Past Rush Hill Farm, etc.
If you wish to avoid this, go straight ahead at Point C and re-join the main route at Point G, just before entering Bampton. We mention this as our moorland route has at least five gates to be opened (and closed again please). We think that the quiet, open road, and the broad views over to the east more than justifies the effort involved...but the choice is yours.

Bampton
Comfortable little village with a Georgian church, which although much restored by the Victorians, retains its unusual wooden arcading. There are two pleasant oil paintings...of Bishop Gibson of London, who spent his early years at Bampton, and of John Boustead, Master of Bampton Grammar School for 56 years. The school has disappeared, but we liked the Crown and Mitre Inn, just beyond the church, and the graceful red sandstone bridge across the Lowther.

Haweswater
This is no longer a lake, but a reservoir created by Manchester Corporation in 1936. Our diversion passes the unsightly concrete dam, and follows the south eastern shore for four miles (diversion total — 6 miles), passing a hotel and ending at a car park below Harter Fell, close to the southern extremity of Haweswater. There are paths from here, (1) up to Blea Water, a tarn standing at over 1500' and more than 200' deep, and (2) south over the Gatesgarth Pass to link with the northern end of Long Sleddale (see page 21). Mardale church stood near the southern end of the valley and was demolished prior to flooding, along with the vicarage and the old hotel.

Swindale
(Fork right at Point J...total road distance to head of dale...3.5 miles.)
Initially our road is unattractive, with very rough common land, embellished only by a dismal little waterworks building. However after about two miles the road enters the dale proper, and although narrower, it becomes much more attractive. From Swindale Head, there is a path over to Haweswater, part of the old 'Corpse Road', which was used to bring the dead over for burial at Shap.

Shap Abbey
Founded by Premonstratensian canons in the early 13th century, in a rather cramped setting beside the river Lowther (the Cistercians would have picked a more ambitious site). Many of the 13th and 14th century walls survive at low level, but the only really impressive structure is the stout early 16th century tower, with its great west window. However with some imagination and the help of the plan provided, one can visualize the pattern of monastic life and work that persisted here for over three hundred years.

Keld Chapel (see page 19)
Shap (see page 19)

1. Bampton

2. Haweswater

3. Early Summer in Swindale

4. Shap Abbey

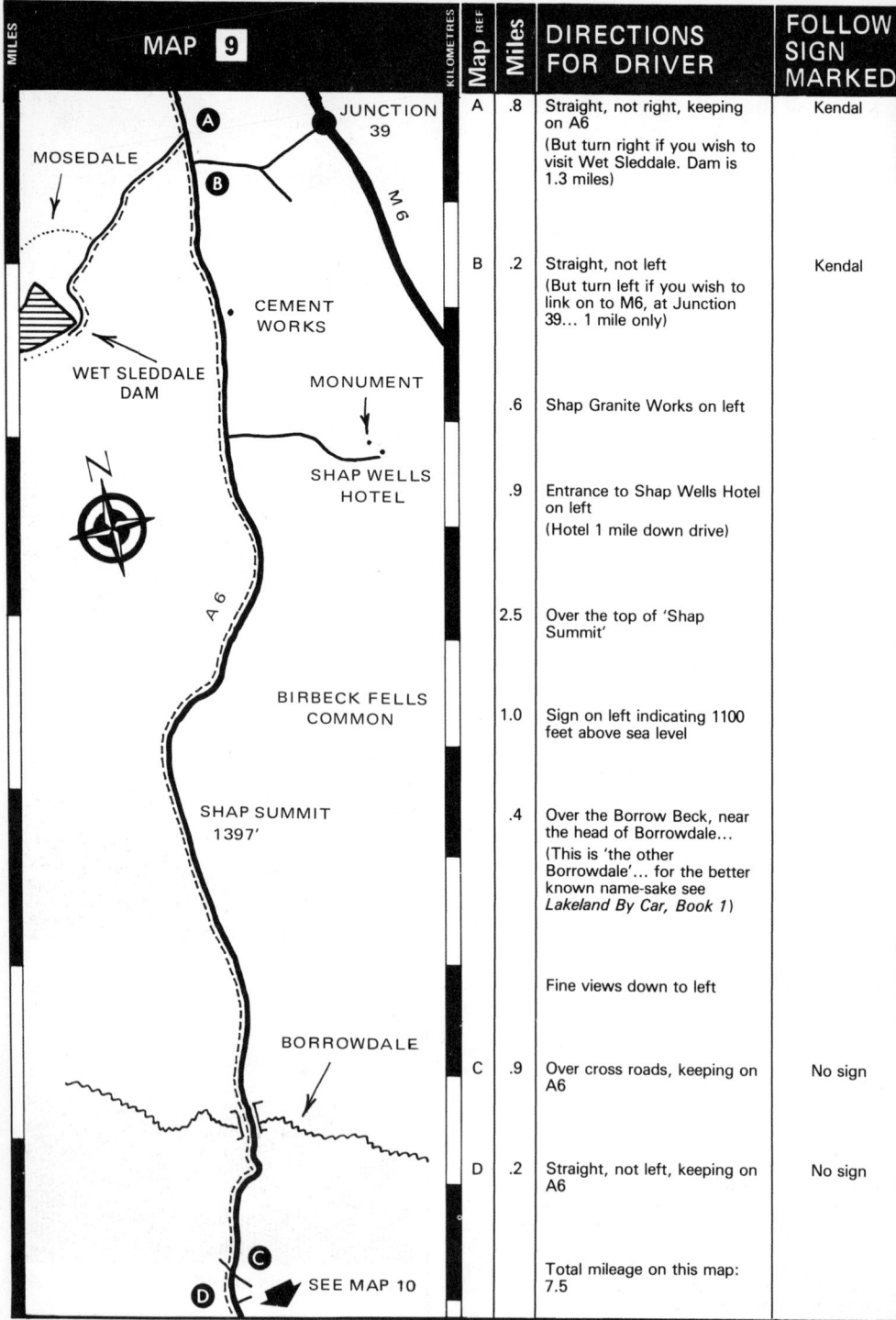

Map REF	Miles	DIRECTIONS FOR DRIVER	FOLLOW SIGN MARKED
A	.8	Straight, not right, keeping on A6 (But turn right if you wish to visit Wet Sleddale. Dam is 1.3 miles)	Kendal
B	.2	Straight, not left (But turn left if you wish to link on to M6, at Junction 39... 1 mile only)	Kendal
	.6	Shap Granite Works on left	
	.9	Entrance to Shap Wells Hotel on left (Hotel 1 mile down drive)	
	2.5	Over the top of 'Shap Summit'	
	1.0	Sign on left indicating 1100 feet above sea level	
	.4	Over the Borrow Beck, near the head of Borrowdale... (This is 'the other Borrowdale'... for the better known name-sake see *Lakeland By Car, Book 1*)	
		Fine views down to left	
C	.9	Over cross roads, keeping on A6	No sign
D	.2	Straight, not left, keeping on A6	No sign
		Total mileage on this map: 7.5	

PLACES OF INTEREST ON THE ROUTE

Keld Chapel (see page 16)

A minute pre-Reformation building with a pleasingly simple interior, which we imagine to be inspired more by post-Reformation ideals. The little stone mullioned east window looks down on a plain altar table. This building is in the care of the National Trust and the key may be obtained from a cottage in the village (see notice on chapel door).

It is possible to walk from Keld south westwards over the fells to Mosedale, and on westwards to link with the Gatesgarth Pass...a path between Haweswater and Long Sleddale. It is also possible to walk westwards up the track, almost to Tailbert Farm, over to Swindale Head (see Swindale on page 17).

1. Wet Sleddale Dam

Shap (see page 16)

A long village, once a popular coaching town, which straggles along the A6. The miniature Market House was built in the late 17th century, and its tiny arches rest upon plump columns...all rather curious. The church is pleasantly sited on higher ground well to the east of the A6, but although it looks interesting enough from the outside, its interior has been over restored by the Victorians.

Wet Sleddale

This dale has been partly flooded by yet another reservoir, and its concrete dam is one of the most depressing structures we have seen in a long time. Manchester Corporation have re-erected an old pack-horse bridge over the Sleddale Beck beyond the head of the reservoir, and one can walk to this from the car park at the end of our 1.3 mile diversion. Further up the valley are two stone enclosures which are thought to have been used for the trapping of deer. They were possibly also used as a releasing point for deer hunting.

It is also possible to walk from our road (see Map) to Mosedale and Gatesgarth Pass (see Keld, above).

2. Shap Wells Hotel

3. The A6 over Shap

Shap Wells Hotel

Pleasant hotel in a hollow below the high fells, about a mile to the left of our road. In the daffodil carpeted woods above the hotel, there is a statue commemorating the accession of Queen Victoria to the throne...a real period piece.

Borrowdale

We cross this dale (not of course to be confused with its better known name sake...see Lakeland by Car, Book 1), at High Borrow Bridge (or Huck's Bridge). There is very little parking space by the bridge, but there is a path down the dale as far as the A685...about 5 miles south-eastward. This is a fine dale, with great sweeping sides, craggy outcrops and scattered woodlands.

4. Borrowdale from the A6

MAP 10

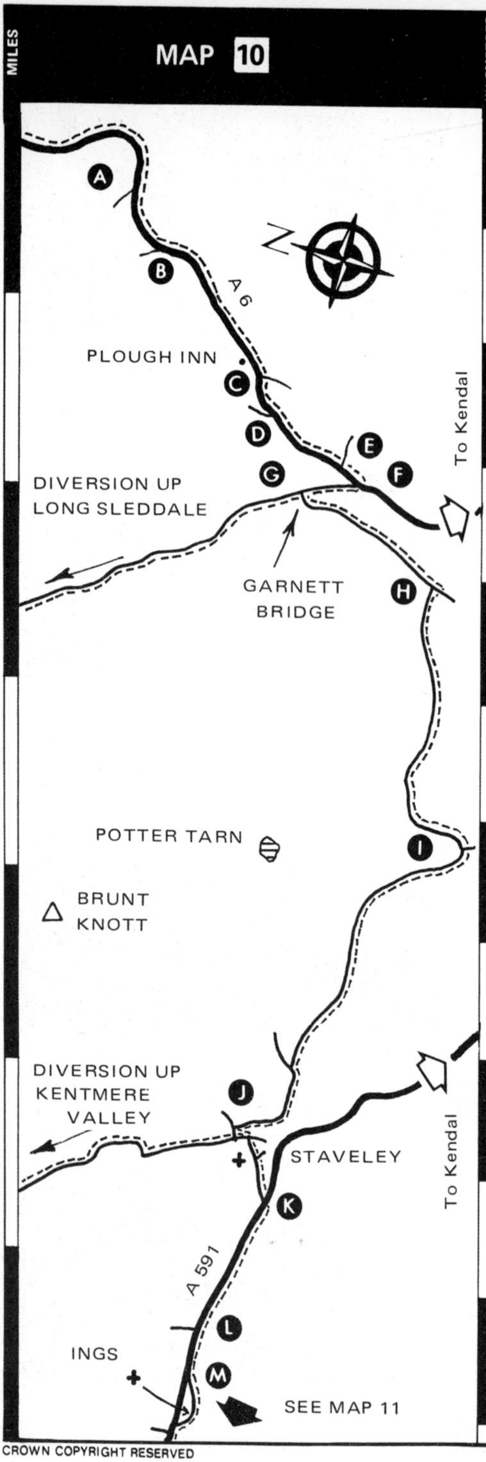

Labels on map:
- PLOUGH INN
- A 6
- To Kendal
- DIVERSION UP LONG SLEDDALE
- GARNETT BRIDGE
- POTTER TARN
- BRUNT KNOTT
- DIVERSION UP KENTMERE VALLEY
- STAVELEY
- To Kendal
- A 591
- INGS
- SEE MAP 11
- CROWN COPYRIGHT RESERVED

Map REF	Miles	DIRECTIONS FOR DRIVER	FOLLOW SIGN MARKED
A	.9	Straight, not right	No sign
B	.3	Straight, not right	No sign
	.7	Plough Inn on right	
C	.1	Straight, not left	Kendal
D	.2	Straight, not right	No sign
E	.4	Straight, not left	Kendal
F	.2	Turn very sharp right, with care, leaving A6	Long Sleddale
		Road now very narrow	
G	.4	Turn left at T junction, and over Garnett Bridge (But go straight ahead if you wish to explore up Long Sleddale . . . 4.6 miles by road)	Burnside
H	.8	Turn right at T junction	No sign
		Pleasant views out over Kendal to left	
I	1.5	Turn right at T junction in woods	Staveley
	.7	River Kent now to left, beyond wall	
		Pleasantly wooded banks	
	.7	Straight, not right at Y junction	No sign
J	.4	Turn left at entry to Staveley, and . . .	No sign
		Over bridge crossing River Kent, and . . .	
	.1	Turn left beyond bridge (But turn right if you wish to explore up the Kentmere Valley . . . 4 miles by road)	No sign
	.1	Turn right by war memorial	No sign
		Church on immediate right	
	.1	Bear right at Y junction	No sign
K	.3	Bear right on to A591	No sign
	.7	Ings entry signed	
L	.1	Straight, not right	No sign
M	.3	Turn left, off A591 beyond petrol station	No sign
		Ings church on immediate right	
	.1	Turn left, re-joining A591	No sign
	.1	Straight, not right, keeping on A591	Windermere
		Total mileage on this map: 9.2	

PLACES OF INTEREST ON THE ROUTE

Long Sleddale
This 4.6 mile diversion is well worth doing but the road is narrow, and out of season days are recommended. After about 1.4 miles Yewbarrow Hall is briefly visible up right...this is in effect a medieval pele tower (see page 7), with cottage attached. A short distance beyond is Long Sleddale church, a small Victorian building, looking out over the Sprint. Inside there is a list of ministers going back to 1670, an old alms chest (1719), and a photograph of the parish's lovely 16th century chalice and cover. At the end of our road is the hamlet of Sadgill, with its beautifully simple, stone bridge, providing a perfect foreground to the ascending valley beyond. One can walk on up here, over the Gatesgarth Pass, to Haweswater (see page 17), to Swindale (see page 17), or to Wet Sleddale (see page 19). Cross Sadgill Bridge, and head south west up the hillside for the bridle-way across to the Kentmere Valley (see below)

Kentmere Valley
This 4 mile diversion is also well worth tackling and furthermore the road is not as narrow as Long Sleddale's. After 3.1 miles beyond Point J there are alternatives:
(1) FORK LEFT for Kentmere church, a pleasant, partly Victorian building, perched high above the marshy valley floor. There is a good 16th century roof and one can truly 'lift up one's eyes unto the hills', looking through the unspoilt plain glass of the east window. Beyond the church is Kentmere Hall, a ruined pele tower, with a 15th century house attached.
(2) FORK RIGHT for a steep mountain road about a mile in length. Park on the right, just short of Brockstones hamlet. Walk eastwards over the bridle-way to Sadgill in Long Sleddale, or up the Kentmere valley to Kentmere reservoir. Splendid views up valley from our car park encompassing the crags of Scale Knotts.

Staveley
Most of this village, including an isolated 14th century church tower, lies on the busy A591. The new church was built in 1864, and although generally rather uninteresting, contains a beautiful window designed by Sir Edward Burne-Jones, and made by the glass works of his friend William Morris.

Ings Church
A handsome building put up in 1743, by Robert Bateman, who was born in the parish, and who grew rich as a merchant in far away Leghorn. Wordsworth's well known epitaph to him, in brass, concludes...
  '...and at his birthplace built a chapel floored with marble which he sent from foreign lands'.
Sadly Bateman never saw the church he paid for, as he was murdered while on his way home to England.

1. Sadgill Bridge, Long Sleddale

2. Track beyond Sadgill Bridge

3. Weir at Staveley

4. View from Kentmere Churchyard

MAP 11

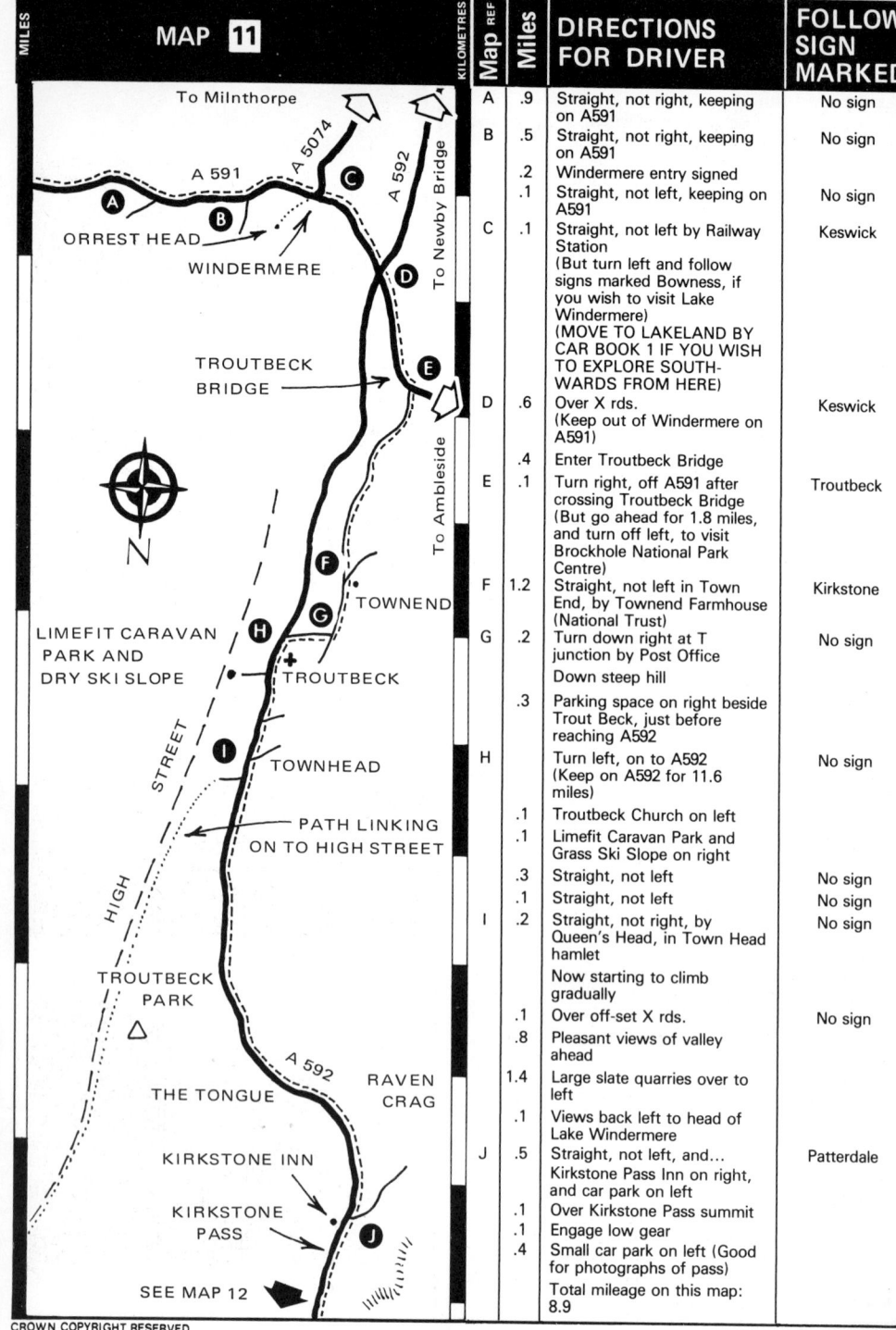

Map REF	Miles	DIRECTIONS FOR DRIVER	FOLLOW SIGN MARKED
A	.9	Straight, not right, keeping on A591	No sign
B	.5	Straight, not right, keeping on A591	No sign
	.2	Windermere entry signed	
	.1	Straight, not left, keeping on A591	No sign
C	.1	Straight, not left by Railway Station (But turn left and follow signs marked Bowness, if you wish to visit Lake Windermere) (MOVE TO LAKELAND BY CAR BOOK 1 IF YOU WISH TO EXPLORE SOUTH-WARDS FROM HERE)	Keswick
D	.6	Over X rds. (Keep out of Windermere on A591)	Keswick
	.4	Enter Troutbeck Bridge	
E	.1	Turn right, off A591 after crossing Troutbeck Bridge (But go ahead for 1.8 miles, and turn off left, to visit Brockhole National Park Centre)	Troutbeck
F	1.2	Straight, not left in Town End, by Townend Farmhouse (National Trust)	Kirkstone
G	.2	Turn down right at T junction by Post Office Down steep hill	No sign
	.3	Parking space on right beside Trout Beck, just before reaching A592	
H		Turn left, on to A592 (Keep on A592 for 11.6 miles)	No sign
	.1	Troutbeck Church on left	
	.1	Limefit Caravan Park and Grass Ski Slope on right	
	.3	Straight, not left	No sign
	.1	Straight, not left	No sign
I	.2	Straight, not right, by Queen's Head, in Town Head hamlet	No sign
		Now starting to climb gradually	
	.1	Over off-set X rds.	No sign
	.8	Pleasant views of valley ahead	
	1.4	Large slate quarries over to left	
	.1	Views back left to head of Lake Windermere	
J	.5	Straight, not left, and... Kirkstone Pass Inn on right, and car park on left	Patterdale
	.1	Over Kirkstone Pass summit	
	.1	Engage low gear	
	.4	Small car park on left (Good for photographs of pass)	
		Total mileage on this map: 8.9	

CROWN COPYRIGHT RESERVED

PLACES OF INTEREST ON THE ROUTE

Windermere (town)
Busy holiday centre which blossomed soon after the arrival of the railway in 1847. Its architecture is therefore inevitably Victorian, but like Bowness it is well endowed with hotels, restaurants, shops and garages, and makes an excellent centre for Lakeland exploration. Orrest Head (784') is easily reached by a footpath starting opposite the station (Point C), and there are fine views from here of Lake Windermere, with Langdale Pikes and Scafell in the background.

Bowness
A continuation of Windermere town, Bowness is beautifully situated on Lake Windermere, about half way down its eastern shore. This is *the* boating centre for England's busiest lake, and at the height of the season, has over 1500 craft upon its waters. The Old England Hotel looks out over the comings and goings of rowing boats, sailing dinghies, cabin cruisers and passenger steamers; and close by stands Bowness church. This has a solidly medieval exterior, but the white painted interior has been overzealously restored by those prosperous Victorians. However do not overlook the 15th century glass in the east window, which probably came from Cartmel Priory and Furness Abbey. Do not miss a visit to the fascinating Windermere Steamboat Museum, half a mile to the north of Bowness, on the lake shore.

Lake District National Park Centre, Brockhole
The house contains an imaginative audio-visual exhibition on all aspects of the Lake District, supported by regular film and slide presentations on topics ranging from Geology and Natural History to Wordsworth. Thirty acres of beautiful gardens stretch down to the lake shore where there is a self-guiding nature walk. Other facilities include a dry-stone wall building area, terrace cafeteria, picnic sites, and children's play area. There is ample parking. Admission charge, but do not miss a visit here.

Townend, Troutbeck
This is regarded as a typical Lake District yeoman farmer's (or statesman's) house... white painted, with stone mullioned windows, and stout round chimneys. It was built about 1626, and was lived in continuously by the Browne family from that date until 1944, it being given to the National Trust four years later. It contains carved woodwork, and the books, papers and furniture collected by the Browne family over the years, and is full of atmosphere and interest. Do not overlook the curious old barn opposite, nor the fine views out over the Troutbeck valley.

Troutbeck
An attractive village scattered along the western slopes of the Troutbeck valley, it being nearly a mile and a half between Town End and Town Head. The
continued on page 29

Kirkstone Pass (see page 29)

1. Jetties at Bowness

2. Townend, Troutbeck

3. Troutbeck Church

4. Kirkstone Pass

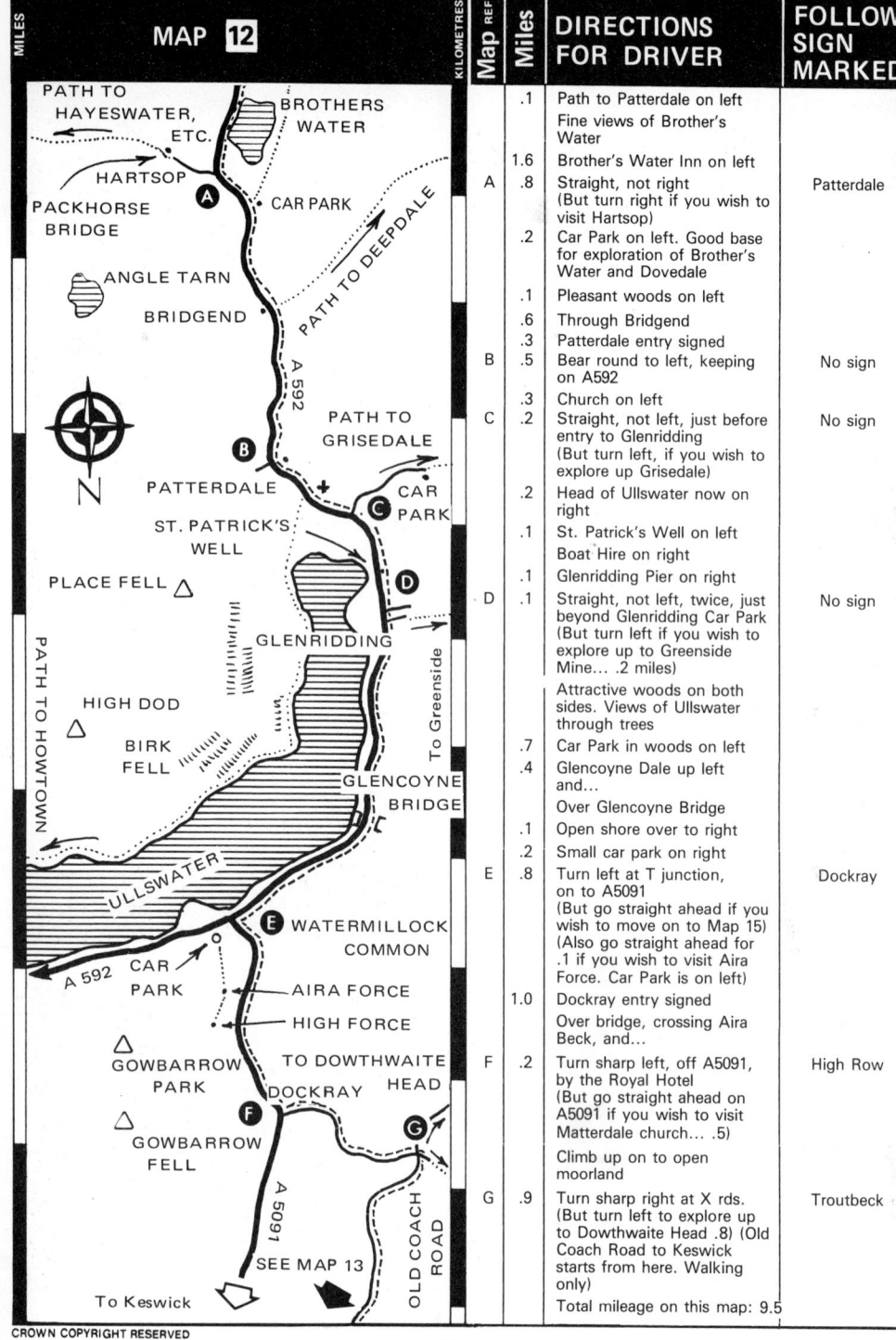

MAP 12

Map REF	Miles	DIRECTIONS FOR DRIVER	FOLLOW SIGN MARKED
	.1	Path to Patterdale on left Fine views of Brother's Water	
	1.6	Brother's Water Inn on left	
A	.8	Straight, not right (But turn right if you wish to visit Hartsop)	Patterdale
	.2	Car Park on left. Good base for exploration of Brother's Water and Dovedale	
	.1	Pleasant woods on left	
	.6	Through Bridgend	
	.3	Patterdale entry signed	
B	.5	Bear round to left, keeping on A592	No sign
	.3	Church on left	
C	.2	Straight, not left, just before entry to Glenridding (But turn left, if you wish to explore up Grisedale)	No sign
	.2	Head of Ullswater now on right	
	.1	St. Patrick's Well on left Boat Hire on right	
	.1	Glenridding Pier on right	
D	.1	Straight, not left, twice, just beyond Glenridding Car Park (But turn left if you wish to explore up to Greenside Mine... .2 miles)	No sign
		Attractive woods on both sides. Views of Ullswater through trees	
	.7	Car Park in woods on left	
	.4	Glencoyne Dale up left and...	
		Over Glencoyne Bridge	
	.1	Open shore over to right	
	.2	Small car park on right	
E	.8	Turn left at T junction, on to A5091 (But go straight ahead if you wish to move on to Map 15) (Also go straight ahead for .1 if you wish to visit Aira Force. Car Park is on left)	Dockray
	1.0	Dockray entry signed	
		Over bridge, crossing Aira Beck, and...	
F	.2	Turn sharp left, off A5091, by the Royal Hotel (But go straight ahead on A5091 if you wish to visit Matterdale church... .5)	High Row
		Climb up on to open moorland	
G	.9	Turn sharp right at X rds. (But turn left to explore up to Dowthwaite Head .8) (Old Coach Road to Keswick starts from here. Walking only)	Troutbeck
		Total mileage on this map: 9.5	

CROWN COPYRIGHT RESERVED

PLACES OF INTEREST ON THE ROUTE

Brother's Water
This small lake comes into view from the lower, northern slopes of the Kirkstone Pass. It is a beautifully tranquil place, overlooked from the south and west by Dove Crag, and the crags of Fairfield and Helvellyn, and from the north, by Place Fell. It is possible to walk up between Brother's Water and Low Wood, past Hartsop Hall, into Dovedale (see Route Directions...Car Park beyond Point A).

Hartsop
Interesting little blue slate hamlet having at least three houses with spinning galleries beneath their overhanging eaves. Immediately beyond the hamlet (only .3 from Point A) there is a car park overlooking an old pack-horse bridge. There are fine views from here up to Hartsop Dodd and Gray Crag, and it is possible to walk up the Hayeswater Gill to Hayeswater itself beneath the crags of High Street (see page 29).

Deepdale
It is possible to walk up from Bridgend, as far as Link Cove, beneath Hart Crag, but do not attempt to "scramble" out of Deepdale unless you are an experienced climber.

Patterdale
Small village on the A592, not far from the head of Ullswater. Its church has a pleasing little saddleback tower, but the interior is not of interest to visitors. It has friendly hotels and shops, and makes an excellent base for walkers and climbers. There are paths...
1. South-west to Angle Tarn,
2. North-west along the shore of Ullswater to Howtown (see also page 31).
3. Up Grisedale to Grisedale Tarn.
4. Up Helvellyn.

(These last two may best be started from the car parking area in Grisedale... Turn left at Point C.)

Glenridding
This is best known as the south-western terminal of the Ullswater 'steamer' service. This service operates between here and Pooley Bridge (see page 31), and also calls at Howtown (see page 31). It is also possible to hire sailing dinghies here. By turning left at Point D, one can drive 1.5 miles up a narrow road, to park below the disused Greenside Mine. This also makes a good starting point for an exploration of the Helvellyn range, but only for those with adequate experience and equipment.

Ullswater
Over seven miles long, and second only in size to Windermere, Ullswater is one of our favourite lakes. It has splendid woodlands (Glencoyne) along its shore beyond Glenridding; and at Glencoyne Bridge, and several miles beyond, there is an open shoreline with several points of access from the road (see also page 31)

Aira Force & Gowbarrow Park (see page 31)
Dockray, Matterdale Church, Dowthwaite Head (see page 27)

1. Hartsop Bridge

2. Ullswater from Glencoyne Woods

3. Ullswater

4. Aira Force   *5. High Force*

MAP 13

Map REF	Miles	DIRECTIONS FOR DRIVER	FOLLOW SIGN MARKED
A	1.6	Bear left, re-joining A5091	No sign
B	1.7	Turn left, off A5091, by 22 Ton Limit Sign at entry to 'Troutbeck Station' hamlet (BUT GO STRAIGHT AHEAD TO LINK ON TO MAP 6, POINT G, TURNING RIGHT, ON TO A66)	No sign
	.9	Over bridge crossing course of old railway	
	.2	'The Bog' on right	
	.6	Dramatic Bannerdale Crags away over to right	
C	.1	Straight, not left	No sign
	.4	Through gate just beyond Wallthwaite hamlet	
	.3	Over cattle-grid, and...	
D	.4	Turn left on to wider road	No sign
		Straight, not left, and...	No sign
E	.1	Turn left on to A66 with care	Keswick
F	.1	Straight, not right twice, keeping on A66 (White Horse Inn, Scale hamlet, up to right)	No sign
G	.7	Straight, not left, keeping on A66	No sign
		Fine views ahead of the Derwent Fells	
H	.7	Turn right, off A66, and into Threlkeld	Threlkeld
	.1	Horse & Farrier Inn on right	
	.1	Church on left	
I	.1	Bear left at T junction	No sign
	.1	Straight, not left	No sign
J	.2	Fork left, keeping on wider road	No sign
K	.1	Turn right WITH CARE on to A66, and almost immediately...	Keswick
		Turn left, off A66	'Stone Circle'
	.1	Pleasant views on left, to Vale of St. John	
L	.7	Straight, not left (But turn left if you wish to explore down to St. John's Church... see opposite for details)	No sign
M	.1	Turn left, off wider road	'Stone Circle'
N	.2	Turn left at T junction	'Castlerigg Stone Circle'
	.6	Castlerigg Stone Circle on left	
O		Straight, not left, beyond Stone Circle	No sign
		NOT SHOWN ON MAP BEYOND THIS POINT	
	.2	Keswick entry signed	
P	.5	Bear left with care on to wider road, and almost immediately...	Town Centre
	.4	Turn right on to A591	Town Centre
		Under railway bridge	
Q	.3	Bear left by County Hotel and memorial	Town Centre
R	.1	Turn right by Royal Oak Hotel	No sign
S	.1	Arrive Moot Hall, Keswick (LINK HERE WITH MAP 1, POINT A)	
		Total mileage on this map: 11.9	

CROWN COPYRIGHT RESERVED

PLACES OF INTEREST ON THE ROUTE

Dockray (see page 24)
Hamlet on the A5091, with the Royal Hotel, a modest establishment overlooking a small bridge over the Aira Beck (all at Map 12, Point F).

Matterdale Church (see page 24)
(Diversion from Map 12, Point F... go straight ahead on A5091 for .5... church is on right.)
Delightful little church, essentially a long low 'dale chapel', but with a tower lovingly added (with great effect) as late as 1848. It has a Jacobean altar rail, an early 18th century two decker pulpit, and entrancing views back over Gowbarrow.

1. Our Road to Scales

The Old Coach Road to Keswick (see page 24)
Keeping at approximately 1400' for some miles, this road, now only a rough track, and charmingly marked 'Unsuitable for Motors', skirts beneath the northern slopes of Matterdale Common, only returning to 'civilization' in the Vale of St. John (see below). There are fine views northwards to Blencathra and Skiddaw.

Scales
A hamlet below the south-eastern slopes of Blencathra (2847'), with a hospitable little inn, the White Horse, just above the busy A66. Apart from various routes up Blencathra, there is a pleasant walking route... up the little road towards Mungrisdale, for about half a mile, turn left, up Mousthwaite Comb, and then up the Glenderamackin valley, to Mungrisdale (see page 13).

2. Cottages at Threlkeld

Threlkeld
Pleasant little village, mercifully by-passed by the hectic A66. The Horse and Farrier Inn, is dated 1688, and both this and the Salutation Inn are cheerful places, much frequented by climbers and fell walkers bound for Blencathra and the long walk north-westwards over Skiddaw Forest, via Skiddaw House and Whitewater Dash (see pages 9 and 13). Skiddaw itself is probably best tackled from Millbeck, near Keswick (see page 29). Threlkeld church was built in 1777, although the unusual little squashed tower is probably 17th century in origin. The panelling behind the altar also incorporates the organ, and the whole 'unit' is contemporary with the church itself. We liked the handsome tablet to the Rev. Thomas Edmundson (1797).

3. Monument at Threlkeld   4. Monument at Threlkeld

St. John's in the Vale
(Turn left at Point L, and turn right after about 1 mile... St. John's church is then on left after a further mile.)
Minute Victorian church standing in trees, on a ridge between St. John's Vale and Nadder Vale. Its delightful setting is enough to make the diversion worthwhile.

Castlerigg Stone Circle
Bronze Age stone circle, about a hundred feet in diameter. The stones are irregular in shape, but their setting is superb, with Latrigg and Blencathra towering over them to the north, and with splendid views over towards Castlerigg Fell and the Derwent Fells, to the south and south-west respectively.

5. Castlerigg Stone Circle

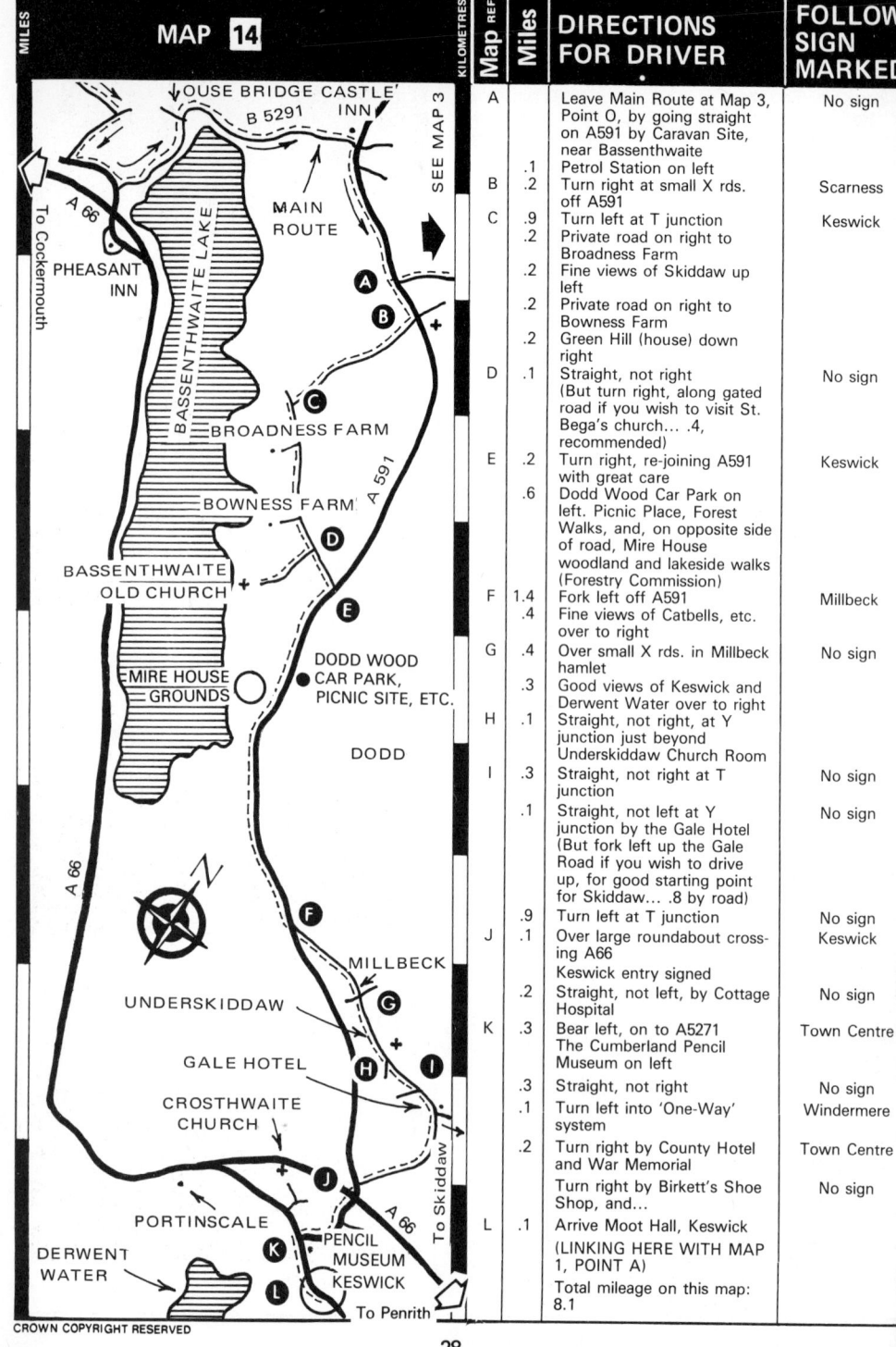

MAP 14

Map Ref	Miles	DIRECTIONS FOR DRIVER	FOLLOW SIGN MARKED
A		Leave Main Route at Map 3, Point O, by going straight on A591 by Caravan Site, near Bassenthwaite	No sign
	.1	Petrol Station on left	
B	.2	Turn right at small X rds. off A591	Scarness
C	.9	Turn left at T junction	Keswick
	.2	Private road on right to Broadness Farm	
	.2	Fine views of Skiddaw up left	
	.2	Private road on right to Bowness Farm	
	.2	Green Hill (house) down right	
D	.1	Straight, not right (But turn right, along gated road if you wish to visit St. Bega's church... .4, recommended)	No sign
E	.2	Turn right, re-joining A591 with great care	Keswick
	.6	Dodd Wood Car Park on left. Picnic Place, Forest Walks, and, on opposite side of road, Mire House woodland and lakeside walks (Forestry Commission)	
F	1.4	Fork left off A591	Millbeck
	.4	Fine views of Catbells, etc. over to right	
G	.4	Over small X rds. in Millbeck hamlet	No sign
	.3	Good views of Keswick and Derwent Water over to right	
H	.1	Straight, not right, at Y junction just beyond Underskiddaw Church Room	
I	.3	Straight, not right at T junction	No sign
	.1	Straight, not left at Y junction by the Gale Hotel (But fork left up the Gale Road if you wish to drive up, for good starting point for Skiddaw... .8 by road)	No sign
	.9	Turn left at T junction	No sign
J	.1	Over large roundabout crossing A66	Keswick
		Keswick entry signed	
	.2	Straight, not left, by Cottage Hospital	No sign
K	.3	Bear left, on to A5271 The Cumberland Pencil Museum on left	Town Centre
	.3	Straight, not right	No sign
	.1	Turn left into 'One-Way' system	Windermere
	.2	Turn right by County Hotel and War Memorial	Town Centre
		Turn right by Birkett's Shoe Shop, and...	No sign
L	.1	Arrive Moot Hall, Keswick (LINKING HERE WITH MAP 1, POINT A)	
		Total mileage on this map: 8.1	

PLACES OF INTEREST ON THE ROUTE

Bassenthwaite Old Church (St. Bega's)
We were delighted with the quiet way down to St. Bega's, with great oak trees beside the track, and the sparkling waters of Bassenthwaite not far away. It is sheltered beneath the massive western shoulder of Skiddaw, and looks across Bassenthwaite to the wooded slopes of Wythop.

The exterior of the church leads us to expect severe Victorianism within, but all turns out to be most charming. There is a Norman chancel arch, a south aisle with broad arcading, and a handsome monument to Walter Vane, inscribed as follows: "Mortally wounded at the Battle of Bayonne, 14th April 1814. Died on 19th of the same month in the 19th year of his age"... a severe statement of fact, which underlines for us the stupidity of human conflict, especially when encountered in so tranquil a setting.

Millbeck
A hamlet beneath the hills, which is probably the easiest starting point for climbing Skiddaw. (By using the Gale Road for about .8 miles... see Route Directions.) (Experienced fell walkers only.)

High Street (see page 14)
From the Roman fort at Brougham, just outside Penrith, a Roman road, now called High Street, ran south-westwards over the fells to Troutbeck, and almost certainly linked on to the road running westwards from Galava, the Roman fort outside Ambleside, to Ravenglass, via the Wrynose and Hardknott passes (see *Lakeland by Car Book 1*). High Street is most unusual, in that it runs for several miles over high mountains (above 2000'), and has resulted in part of the range itself being called High Street. It is possible to walk south-west, up the drive of Winder Hall Farm (.1 beyond Point O), and within two miles, the course of the 'road' is already over a thousand feet above sea level (close to a reasonably well defined stone circle on Moor Divock). (Experienced fell walkers only.)

Troutbeck *continued from page 23*
church is situated beside the busy main road in the valley. It has some fine Jacobean panelling, which came from Calgarth Hall, Windermere, and an interesting east window, partly designed by Sir Edward Burne-Jones and partly by Ford Madox-Brown, and made at the glass works of their friend William Morris.

Kirkstone Pass (see page 22)
At 1476', this is the highest and longest pass in the Lake District, but when compared with the Honister, Wrynose or Hardknott (see Book 1), it is one of the easiest. However parts of the descent are as steep as 1 in 4, and considerable care should be taken. The Pass leads between the dramatic Red Screes and Raven Crags on the west, and the less pronounced heights of Caudale Moor on the east. The Kirkstone Pass Inn, at 1468' is England's third highest pub... Tan Hill in Yorkshire is highest at 1727', and the Cat & Fiddle in Derbyshire is second at 1690'.

1. Near Bassenthwaite Old Church

2. Bassenthwaite Old Church

3. View from Underskiddaw

4. The Moot Hall, Keswick

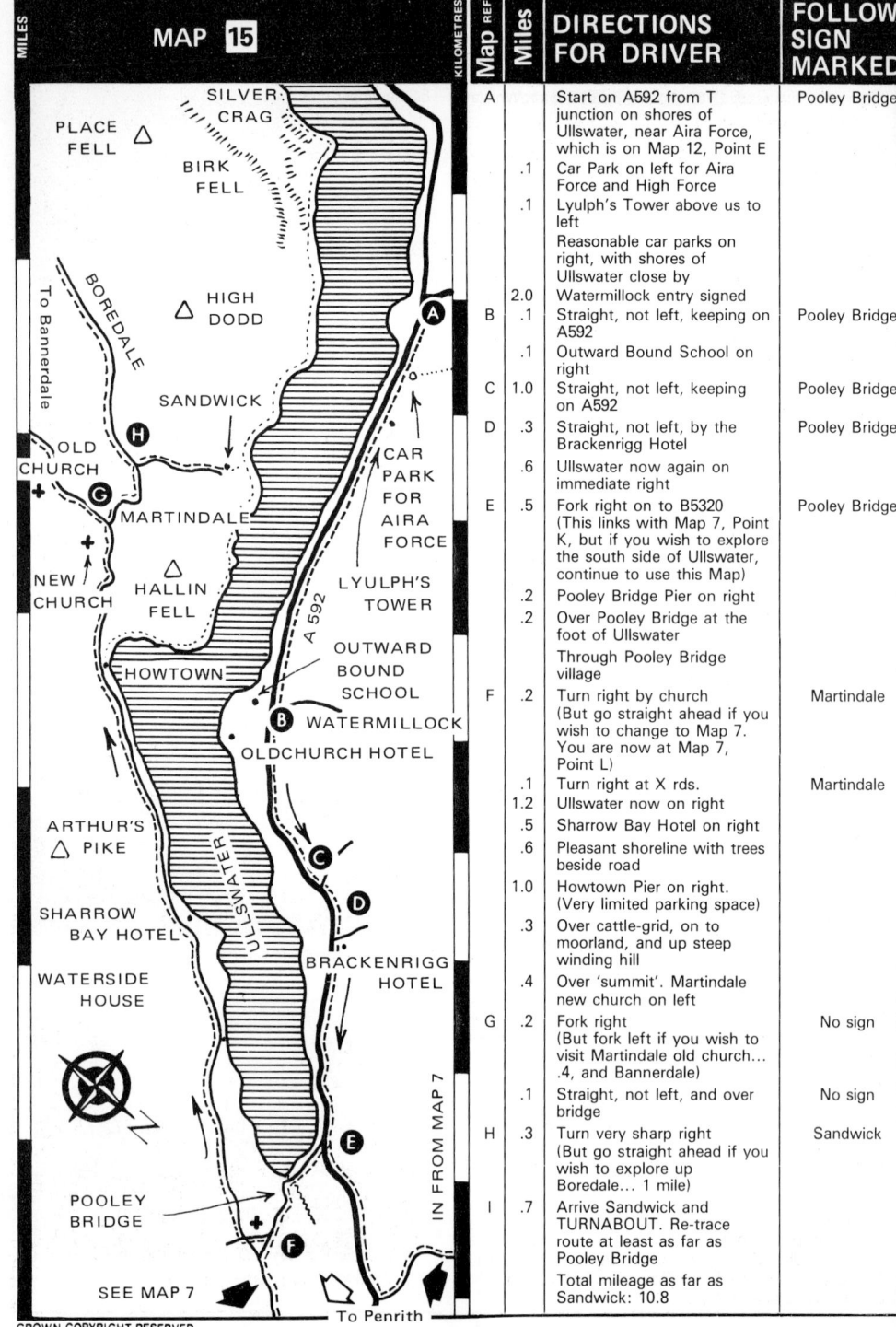

Map ref	Miles	DIRECTIONS FOR DRIVER	FOLLOW SIGN MARKED
A		Start on A592 from T junction on shores of Ullswater, near Aira Force, which is on Map 12, Point E	Pooley Bridge
	.1	Car Park on left for Aira Force and High Force	
	.1	Lyulph's Tower above us to left	
	2.0	Reasonable car parks on right, with shores of Ullswater close by Watermillock entry signed	
B	.1	Straight, not left, keeping on A592	Pooley Bridge
	.1	Outward Bound School on right	
C	1.0	Straight, not left, keeping on A592	Pooley Bridge
D	.3	Straight, not left, by the Brackenrigg Hotel	Pooley Bridge
	.6	Ullswater now again on immediate right	
E	.5	Fork right on to B5320 (This links with Map 7, Point K, but if you wish to explore the south side of Ullswater, continue to use this Map)	Pooley Bridge
	.2	Pooley Bridge Pier on right	
	.2	Over Pooley Bridge at the foot of Ullswater	
		Through Pooley Bridge village	
F	.2	Turn right by church (But go straight ahead if you wish to change to Map 7. You are now at Map 7, Point L)	Martindale
	.1	Turn right at X rds.	Martindale
	1.2	Ullswater now on right	
	.5	Sharrow Bay Hotel on right	
	.6	Pleasant shoreline with trees beside road	
	1.0	Howtown Pier on right. (Very limited parking space)	
	.3	Over cattle-grid, on to moorland, and up steep winding hill	
	.4	Over 'summit'. Martindale new church on left	
G	.2	Fork right (But fork left if you wish to visit Martindale old church... .4, and Bannerdale)	No sign
	.1	Straight, not left, and over bridge	No sign
H	.3	Turn very sharp right (But go straight ahead if you wish to explore up Boredale... 1 mile)	Sandwick
I	.7	Arrive Sandwick and TURNABOUT. Re-trace route at least as far as Pooley Bridge	
		Total mileage as far as Sandwick: 10.7	

CROWN COPYRIGHT RESERVED

PLACES OF INTEREST ON THE ROUTE

Aira Force and Gowbarrow Park
This delightful area is all in the care of the National Trust, and should be explored from the car park at Aira Green. There is a good map of the best walks displayed at the car park, and an excellent leaflet (*Two Walks from Aira Green*) published by the Lake District National Park. Aira Force itself is a sixty foot high waterfall in a wooded valley, with little stone bridges immediately above and below it. There are splendid views from Yew Crag, and the summits of Gowbarrow Park and Gowbarrow Fell, out over Ullswater to High Dod and Place Fell. The waterfall of High Force lies above Aira Force, but is less dramatic.

1. Ullswater, from Oldchurch

Lyulph's Tower
A late 18th century hunting lodge, built by the Duke of Norfolk in the style of a medieval castle, with towers and curtain walls forming three sides of an octagon. This is a fascinating example of a 'folly' being built for a definite purpose. It is private property, standing in private grounds.

Pooley Bridge (See also page 14)
A pleasantly busy village at the north-eastern end of Ullswater, with a pier from which a steamer service operates in summertime to Glenridding, a small Victorian church, brightly painted shops, and a cheerful hotel, the Crown.

2. Sharrow Bay, Ullswater

Howtown
This lies on the south-eastern shore of Ullswater, and is reached by a beautiful lake-side road from Pooley Bridge. The lake steamers plying between Glenridding and Pooley Bridge call at Howtown Pier, and although parking space in the immediate vicinity is limited, a lake journey could be taken from here to Glenridding, and one could then walk back to Howtown along the shore (see National Parks Leaflet... *Two Walks from Glenridding*).

Martindale
A steep, but very attractive serpentine road leads up out of Howtown, over a miniature pass to Martindale. Its 'new' church has a nicely painted reredos, but is otherwise rather uninteresting. The old church is a typical 'dale chapel', and was built in 1633. It is a simple building with low roof, an altar table dated 1674, and a pleasing lectern contemporary with the church. Do not miss this most attractive little building.

3. Martindale Old Church

Boredale (or Boardale)
This, like Martindale and Bannerdale, has fine sweeping flanks, and it is possible to walk beyond the road's end at Dale Head, up over the spur between Place Fell and Angle Tarn Pikes, and down to Patterdale and Glenridding.

Sandwick
Lies on the path between Howtown and Glenridding and marks the end of this enchanting five and a half mile diversion from Pooley Bridge... a fitting end to our Lakeland journey.

4. Journey's End, at Sandwick

INDEX

	Page
Aira Beck	27
Aira Force	24, 31
Aira Green	31
Angle Tarn	25
Angle Tarn Pikes	31
Armathwaite Hall	7
Askham	15
Bampton	17
Bannerdale	31
Bannerdale Crags	26
Bassenthwaite Lake	7, 29
Bassenthwaite Old Church	29
Bateman, Robert	21
Binney Hill	8
Bleaberry Tarn	5
Blea Water	17
Blencathra	3, 27
Boardale	31
Bomby	16
Boredale	31
Borrowdale	19
Borrowdale Fells	3
Boustead, J.	17
Bowness	23
Bowscale (hamlet)	12
Bowscale Fell	13
Bowscale Tarn	13
Brackenthwaite	5
Braithwaite	5
Branthwaite	9
Bridgend	25
Brockhole	23
Brockstones	21
Brother's Water	25
Brougham	15
Burne-Jones, Sir Edward	21, 29
Buttermere	5
Buttermere Hause	3
Caldbeck	11
Caldbeck Fells	9
Caldew, River	10
Caldew Valley	11, 13
Calebrack	13
Carrock Fell	11, 13
Castle Head	3
Castlerigg Fell	27
Castlerigg Stone Circle	27
Castle Sowerby	11
Catbells	3
Caudale Moor	29
Chantrey, Sir Francis	15
Cinderdale Common	5
Cockermouth	7
Cocker, River	7
Coledale Pass	5
Crosthwaite	3
Crummock Water	5
Dacre	15
Dacre Castle	15
Dalemain	15
Dash Falls	9
Deepdale	25
Derwent Fells	27
Derwent, River	7
Derwentwater	3
Dockray	24, 27
Dodd Wood Forest Walks, etc.	28
Dowthwaite Head	24
Dove Crag	25
Dovedale	25
Dubs, River	5
Ellen, River	8
Fairfield	25
Fellside	9

	Page
Fitz Park Museum & Art Gallery	3
Flaxman, J.	23
Forest Visitor Centre, Whinlatter	5
Friar's Crag	3
Galava	15
Gale Road, The	29
Gatesgarth Pass	17, 19, 21
Gibson, Bishop	17
Glenderamackin Valley	13, 27
Glencoyne Bridge	25
Glencoyne Dale	24
Glencoyne Woods	25
Glenridding	25, 31
Gowbarrow	27
Gowbarrow Fell	31
Gowbarrow Park	31
Grasmoor	5
Graves, J. W.	11
Gray Crag	25
Great Gable	5
Great Mell	12
Great Mell Fell	26
Greenhead	8
Greenside Mine	25
Greta, River	2
Grisedale	5, 25
Grisdale Pike	3
Grisedale Tarn	25
Hart Crag	25
Harter Fell	17
Hartsop	25
Hartsop Hall	25
Hause Point	4
Haweswater	17, 21
Hayeswater	25
Helton	16
Helvellyn	25
Hesket Newmarket	11
High Barrow Bridge	19
High Dod	31
High Force	24, 31
High Row	11
High Snockrigg	5
High Spy	3
High Street	25, 29, 31
Hobcarton Pike	5
Howk, The	11
Howtown	25, 31
Huck's Bridge	19
Hutton John	13, 14
Hutton Roof	11
Ings Church	21
Keld Chapel	16, 19
Kendal	20
Kentmere Hall	21
Kentmere Reservoir	21
Kentmere Valley	21
Kent, River	20
Keskadale	3
Keswick	3, 26, 28
Kirkstile	5
Kirkstone Pass	22, 29
Knott Rigg	3
Langdale Pikes	23
Lanthwaite Green	5
Latrigg	27
Lingholm Gardens	3
Link Cove	25
Little Tarn	8
Littletown	3
Long Sleddale	17, 19
Lonsdale, Earl of	15
Lord's Seat	7
Lorton	5

	Page
Lorton Hall	5
Lowther Castle	15
Lowther Church	15
Lowther, River	15, 17
Lowther, Sir James	7
Lowther Wildlife Park	15
Low Wood	23
Lyulph's Tower	31
Madox-Brown, F.	29
Manchester Corporation	17, 19
Mardale Church	17
Martindale	31
Matterdale Church	25, 27
Matterdale Common	27
Mayo, Earl of	7
Mellbreak	5
Millbeck	9, 27, 29
Millhouse (hamlet)	10
Mire House Walks	28
Moor Divock Stone Circle	29
Moot Hall, The	3
Morris, William	21, 29
Mosedale	13
Moss Force	3
Mousthwaite Comb	27
Mungrisdale	13, 27
Nadder Vale	27
National Park Centre, Brockhole	23
Newlands	3
Newlands Hause	3
Nickol End	3
Norfolk, Duke of	31
Old Coach Road	27
Old Corpse Road	17
Orrest Head	23
Orthwaite Hall	9
Ouse Bridge	7
Over Water	8
Park Wood	9
Patterdale	25, 31
Peel, John	11
Pele Towers	7
Penruddock	14
Pheasant Inn, The	7
Place Fell	25, 31
Pooley Bridge	14, 25, 31
Portinscale	3
Rawnsley, Canon	3
Raven Crags	12, 29
Red Screes, The	29
Robinson	3
Rosgill	16
Rush Hill Farm	17
Sadgill	21
Sail Beck	2
St. Bega's Church	29
St. John's in the Vale	27
St. Patrick's Well	24
Sandwick	31
Scafell	23
Scale Force	5
Scale Knotts	21
Scales	13, 27
Scales Fell	13
Scandale	24
Shap	16, 19
Shap Abbey	17
Shap Wells Hotel	19
Sharrow Bay	30
Skiddaw	3, 7, 27, 29
Skiddaw Forest	9, 27
Skiddaw House	9, 13, 27
Smirke, Robert	15
Sour Milk Gill	5